The Technique of GROWING FROM SEED

David Pople

Eric Bruton Associates Ltd, Ipswich, Suffolk

First Published 1985

Illustrations by Janet Skea

ISBN 7198 0004 8 (Hardback)
ISBN 7198 0014 5 (Limp Edition)

Text input by Eric Bruton Associates.
Typeset by Budget Typesetting Ltd., Beckenham, Kent.
Printed in Great Britain by Acolortone Ltd., Ipswich.
Bound by Anchor Brendon Ltd., Tiptree, Colchester, Essex.

Contents

Introduction

The ability to raise plants successfully from seeds is one of the most fascinating and satisfying, as well as important, facets of gardening. It is also one in which all gardeners should aim to become proficient. It is not a difficult accomplishment to master, however, because it is chiefly a matter of developing the right techniques. The really tricky part is done by Nature: all we really have to do is create the right conditions that will allow her to get on with the job. Provided you use a good seed, sow it and look after the seedlings correctly, you should have little trouble in harvesting bumper crops of vegetables or filling your garden with summer flowers. Even if you attempt to raise the more unusual plants, such as shrubs and trees or alpines, you should not have real difficulty if you follow the right method, though it often requires more patience. But the thrill when those first tiny green shoots appear through the soil is an excitement only people who sow unusual seeds can ever experience.

Why bother fussing about with seeds when you can buy plants? This is the common reaction of people who have perhaps been disappointed with their efforts in sowing. Well there are several reasons why it is worth the trouble. Firstly because it is cheap. Anyone would think twice before paying the price of a dozen plants of delphiniums or Oriental poppies these days, but far more than this can be produced from a single packet of seeds in the course of a summer. Then there is a whole host of plants that can only be obtained by growing them from seed. In some cases this is because the only satisfactory way is to sow them where they are to grow: in others they may be plants not in general cultivation and unobtainable except as seeds.

Seedlings have an advantage in that they tend to be more vigorous than plants raised by other means. They usually start off with a clean bill of health also ... an important point where old stocks of some plants, such as lilies, are commonly infected with various diseases which affect their performance. Then again seedlings are the chief source of new varieties that are an advance on older ones. Whatever the reasons you raise them from seed, however, when the plants reach maturity and flower or fruit for the first time there is always an additional feeling of satisfaction in knowing that you raised them yourself.

In this book I hope to dispel some of the mystique surrounding the subject of seedling raising and explain why different plants behave as they do, as well as point out the path to success. Although sowing failures usually bring forth complaints about the quality of the seeds, it is more often a lack of know-how that is the real problem. Yet the actual work involved in raising plants from seed is not in the least difficult. What it does require is attention to detail and doing what is required at the right time. Before going on to the practice, however, we must first have a look at what seeds actually are and their particular needs.

Throughout this book I have used the term seed not according to the strict botanical definition, but in the wider gardener's sense to mean seeds as they are found in a packet or gathered from a plant, in which state they may have an extra protective coat, tuft of hairs or some other attachment on or around what a botanist would regard as the true seed.

1. What are seeds?

Seeds are the dormant young of flowering plants and each one is a little miracle. It seems hard to believe that such unprepossessing, dried up fragments of plant tissue could contain all that is necessary to develop into gorgeous flowering plants, shrubs or trees, or even contain life at all; but they do. In size they can vary from the seeds of certain orchids, a thousand of which could be taken for a pinch of snuff, to that of the double coconut or coco de mer (*Lodoicea maldivica*), a palm native to the Seychelles, whose massive fruits can weigh upwards of 40 lb (18 kg) and usually contain a single seed. But size of seed bears no relation to the size of plant it comes from. Some trees have very small seeds, whereas those of the broad bean, for instance, are quite large.

Seeds also have a seemingly infinite variety of shapes and colours. Some are round like those of the cabbage family, or can be oval, pointed, flat, even stick-like in the case of salsify. Others resemble curled caterpillars or snail shells. They can be black to white through every conceivable shade of brown and cream, bright red or orange and occasionally other colours, sometimes beautifully mottled. So colourful, hard and bead-like are some seeds, in fact, that strings of them are used as necklaces in warm countries.

As well as providing a source of young plants to guarantee the survival of a species, seeds frequently play a major role in widening plant distribution. Some are adapted to floating in water, others, due to their minute size or special appendages, are spread far and wide by wind. Everyone must surely be familiar with a dandelion clock which, when puffed at, releases a crowd of tiny seeds each dangling from a silky parachute that can travel for miles. Then there are seeds which are designed for 'animal transport' having hooks attached that hang on to fur or clothing, or being equipped to survive the passage through the digestive tract of a bird or animal to which they are presented within an attractive fruit or berry.

Whatever their other physical differences, however, all seeds that are viable - that is living and capable of developing into plants - contain a dormant embryo, or the ability to produce one, together with a concentrated supply of food to sustain it in its initial stages of

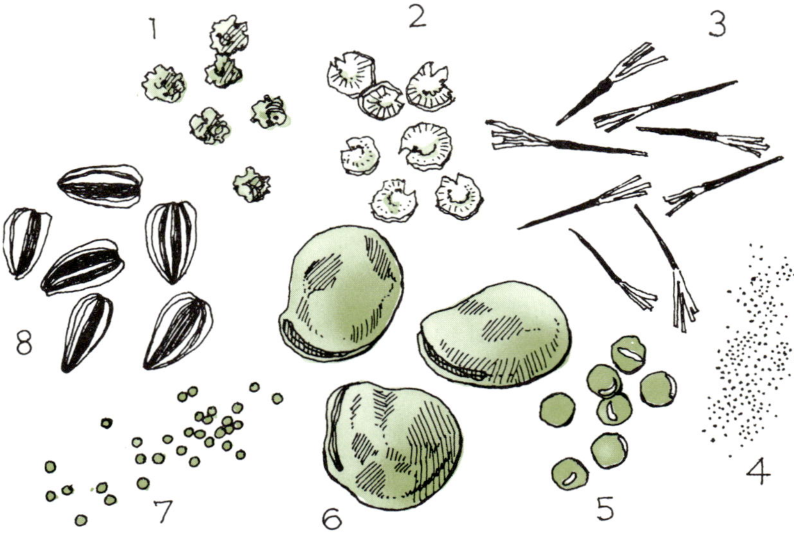

Seeds come in a wide variety of shapes and sizes. Those illustrated here are of: 1. Beetroot. 2. Hollyhock. 3. French Marigold. 4. Lobelia. 5. Sweet Pea. 6. Broad Bean. 7. Cauliflower. 8. Sunflower.

growth, within a protective outer coat. The food may be stored in the form of starch, as in the case of wheat which is ground to make flour, or as an oil such as is found in seeds of the common flax that are the source of linseed oil.

Not every seed produced by a plant is viable, however. Some may have malformed embryos, others none at all. Different species vary in the percentage of viable seeds they can produce and the number may vary according to the season. Plants grown far from their normal habitat may only set viable seed very infrequently, while some hybrids are 'mules' and though they flower abundantly are incapable of producing seeds at all. You should not therefore expect every seed in a packet or gathered from a plant to produce a seedling. But a reputable seedsman will ensure that the viability will be reasonable for the plant concerned. In the case of vegetables the minimum standard of germination for seeds sold is controlled by statute, but even these are not the same for all and run from 85% for rape and cucumber down to 60% for celery and carrot and as low as 55% for tap-rooted Cheltenham varieties of beetroot. I must emphasise, however, that these figures represent the acceptable minimum and not necessarily the usual standard that may be expected.

Length of Life

Seeds vary enormously in their life expectancy. That of willows, for instance, being measured in days rather than weeks, while others can remain viable for many years in the right conditions. A strange example of longevity is provided by the sacred lotus (*Nelumbo nucifera*) some seeds of which, found in Manchuria at the site of what was once a lake, were germinated in America. Subsequent examination showed the seeds may have been over 1,000 years old. But there is no scientific evidence to suggest any truth in the old myth that wheat grains in the tomb of Tutankamen were still viable when found.

Apart from the fact that the seeds of different species have different lengths of life expectancy, the conditions in which they spend their period of dormancy has a great effect for good or ill. Not surprisingly conditions opposite those that encourage germination, namely dryness, low temperature and low oxygen level, are generally best. In the specially low temperature maintained in a seed bank seeds can be held in what seems to be a completely suspended state of animation for years. You will find that the vast majority of seeds bought in packets will keep best in a plastic box in the kitchen refrigerator where the air is cold and dry. In the case of acorns and other large, moist, fleshy or oily seeds, however, excessive desiccation in dry air can quickly reduce their viability. These are best sown in soil as soon as possible where they can be kept moist until such times as they do germinate.

It is lack of oxygen that probably ensures buried seeds remain dormant, rather than coldness, and certainly not lack of moisture. That seeds can survive for a long time in the soil is shown by the way weeds like scarlet corn poppies and yellow charlock can develop in abundance on land ploughed up after it has been under grass for 15 or more years, and appear along the sides of new road works where the soil has been disturbed. It also explains why every time you dig a patch of soil in the garden you get a fresh crop of weeds, and bears out that old gardener's saying, 'One year's seeding, seven year's weeding'. It seems that viable seeds are able to secrete some chemical that protects them from the agents of decay while lying dormant in the soil, though they soon rot when they eventually die.

The rate at which the seeds of different plants lose their viability varies. In some batches the percentage of viable seeds drops over a number of seasons, while others may lose all their powers of regeneration at more or less the same time, rather as though travelling along a plateau together they had come to cliff at the end. There is no way to tell from a purely visual inspection whether dry seeds are living or not. Indeed it is possible for some seeds never to have been viable at all. This is why it pays to buy seeds from a reputable seed firm who check their stocks for viability and, where possible, for germinating ability.

Conditions for Germination

The conditions needed to trigger the reawakening of ordinary seeds are an adequate supply of water, a certain degree of warmth and plenty of oxygen. First the seed absorbs moisture and swells. Its coat is softened and enzymes within it begin to convert the stored food into a form which the embryo can use. With active growth the respiration rate increases (whereas that of dormant seeds is so low as to be undetectable) hence the need for plenty of oxygen. But these activities can only take place in the right temperature range, which varies for different plants. Too much as well as too little warmth can inhibit germination.

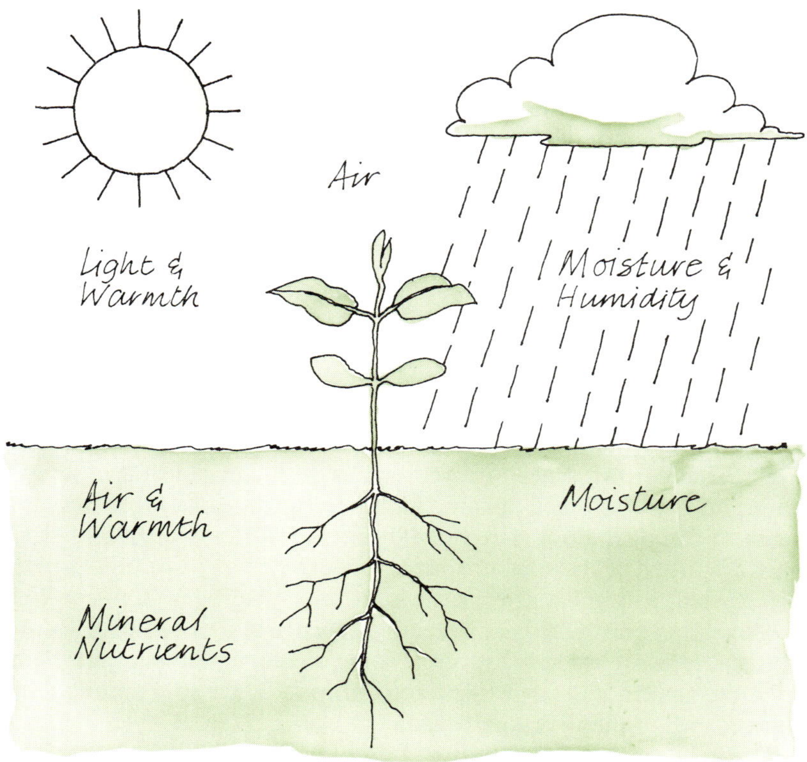

All green plants need an adequate supply of light and air, warmth and moisture as well as food if they are to thrive, all of which are provided by Nature. Moisture and humidity come from rain and dew; light and warmth from the sun. The soil is a storehouse of the many mineral nutrients plants need. Oxygen is as essential to plants as animals, but the atmosphere also provides carbon dioxide which, together with water, green plants use in the manufacture of carbohydrates in their leaves.

Temperature can play a much more important part in germination than many gardeners realise, because plants commonly raised from seed will develop over quite a wide temperature range. But there are plants which only germinate within very narrow limits. However, those plants commonly raised from seed can be broadly divided into three groups for their temperature needs:

1. **Hardy Plants** - those that are grown outdoors and can withstand frost, including such vegetables as cabbage and carrots. These do well in a soil temperature of 55-60F (13-16C).

2. **Half-hardy Plants** - those that can be grown outdoors in summer but which are damaged by frost, including runner beans and marrows. These come from warmer regions and germinate well in the temperature range of 60-70F (16-21C).

3. **Tender Plants** - those that are normally grown in a warm greenhouse or indoors throughout the year. Many come from tropical areas and as you might expect need a brisk heat in the region of 70-75F (21-24C), even as high as 80F (27C) in some instances.

Because of their commercial importance a great deal of research has been applied to vegetable crops. Many will germinate at temperatures as low as 45F (7C) - lettuce when the soil is much colder still - but seedling emergence is bound to be slow at the lower end of the range. On the other hand, the smooth-leaved lettuce varieties are inhibited if the soil temperature goes above 77F (25C), while leeks and onions do not germinate well if the soil is over 70-75F (21-24C).

A drop of some 10F (6C) between day and night temperatures often gives better results with hardy plants and is usually the natural state of affairs out of doors. Many tender plants, like impatiens and zonal pelargoniums need a much more stable temperature regime if they are to germinate well.

Some Special Needs

Once you get away from the usual run of vegetable and flower seeds it is surprising how many of them will germinate in the presence of light. But this seems to be some built-in trigger mechanism because just a tenth of a second of bright light at the right time is enough to do the trick with some seeds. Obviously these should never be buried in the soil at planting time, or if they are covered at all it should be no more than the merest sprinkling of sand that cannot block out the light completely.

Some others, at least when first harvested, will only germinate in complete darkness. But since seeds are normally sown and covered in a bed or pot of soil or compost, where it is easier to keep them moist, this does not normally cause problems to a gardener.

Sometimes the seed coats are so hard as to be impervious to water and a seed can lie dormant in the soil for months, if not years, until this outer layer is finally softened or broken down sufficiently for water to get in. This is often a particular problem with dark-coloured sweet pea seeds, as well as those of cannas (that are commonly called Indian

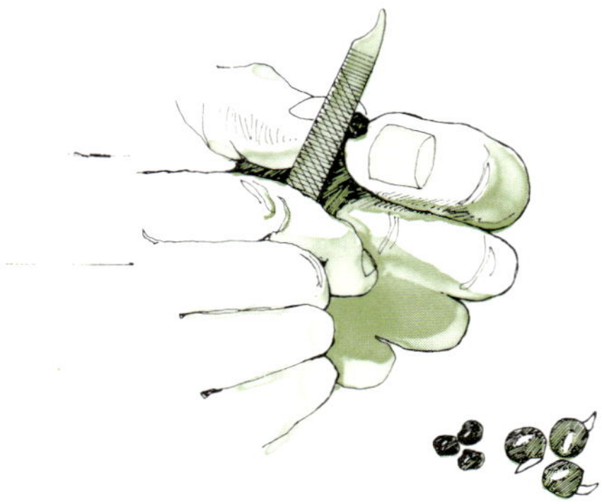

Removing a small piece of the hard outer skin of dark-coloured sweet pea seeds is often needed to allow quick moisture penetration and even germination (lower right).

shot), camellias and some other plants. It can be overcome simply by soaking the seeds for 24 hours beforehand, then filing away a small part of the seed coat with the aid of a nail file on the side opposite the scar of any seed that has failed to swell. This is far safer than trying to do the job with a sharp knife or razor blade as is sometimes suggested. An alternative method is to scarify the dry seeds by rubbing them between two sheets of sandpaper.

Large seeds absorb a surprising quantity of water before germinating as illustrated here. Both glasses contain the same quantity of pea seeds, but those on the right have been soaked over night.

Beet is an oddity among vegetables in that its germination can be delayed by a chemical growth inhibitor. It is impregnated in the knobbly 'seeds' you find in a packet, but which are actually capsules containing several seeds*. If these are sown in dryish soil it is not until rain arrives or the area is watered that the inhibitor is washed away and the seeds can start to grow.

Awkward Customers

Nature is nothing if not ingenious and has devised a variety of ways to ensure that a whole generation of plants is never lost completely. Unfortunately, in this case the interests of Nature and that of the gardener are opposed. While one is trying to stagger germination perhaps, or ensure that it only occurs at the best season, the other wishes to raise plants quickly and effectively when required. The result is that there are a number of awkward customers that test both the skill and patience of anyone who wishes to raise them from seed.

Before going on to look at some of the trickier plants let me hasten to add that this does not apply to the wide range of vegetables and flowering plants commonly offered in seed catalogues and shops. These have largely been bred and selected, sometimes for centuries, to provide quick, even and reliable germination. Once you get the sowing technique right you should have little difficulty in raising them successfully. The closer you get to wild plants, however, the more likely you are to find special cases.

In one sense all seeds are dormant while they are waiting for the right conditions of moisture, warmth and oxygen that will trigger them into growth. But the term 'dormancy' is usually reserved for those seeds that, although viable, fail to respond to these normal stimuli and continue to sleep in the soil. This is by no means uncommon since the dry seeds of many plants need a period of 'after ripening' when they have been gathered or shed by plants before they can germinate, as you will know if you have ever saved your own lettuce seeds and sown them at once. Generally this period is quite

---

*It is now possible to buy beetroot varieties that are what is termed mono-germ and have only one seed in each capsule.

Parsley is often regarded as the slowest of all vegetables to germinate. This can be due to the fact that the seeds may not have fully-formed embryos when harvested. The result is then a delay after sowing while the embryo is completed before the seeds even begin to germinate. The same thing can also happen with seeds of carrot and parsnips, which are related to parsley, and sometimes seem to take an extraordinarily long time to appear. This is especially true of early spring sowings made before the soil is warm enough to speed their growth.

short, perhaps 2-3 months, so by the time you want to sow the seeds in spring or buy them in a packet, it has long gone.

Chilling is One Key

One type of difficulty quite commonly met with is seeds whose embryos remain dormant until they have passed through a cold spell equivalent to a winter period. For example, it is a condition imposed by Nature upon the seeds of some Alpine plants. In that area the plants must grow, flower and produce seeds within a period of some 12-16 weeks, which is the only time they are uncovered by snow. Were the seeds to germinate immediately they were shed, the tiny seedlings would have to face the winter before they had grown large enough to survive. To prevent this the seeds have a germination-inhibitor which is destroyed by a spell of cold. Not until the following winter is their dormancy 'broken' and then they can germinate normally when spring arrives and the seedlings have a whole summer, if a short one, in which to grow before the onset of yet another winter.

The condition has been found to affect not only the seeds of many gentians and other alpine plants, but a number of primula species and other plants, including trees and shrubs. One in particular which has disappointed countless gardeners who have been attracted by its incredibly beautiful blue flowers, is the Himalayan poppy, *Meconopsis betonicifolia (M. baileyi)*. In the case of some plants, including this meconopsis and some primulas, this enforced dormancy is not apparent until the seeds are fully ripened. Provided they have been gathered and sown before they have fully dried the seeds can germinate freely. But if you buy the seeds in a packet you can be sure they will need special treatment.

These seeds are not at all difficult to deal with if you know they behave in this way. All you need to do is to sow them in autumn, or as soon as you can get the seeds, and stand the containers out of doors, or in an open cold frame and leave them exposed to the weather. You must, of course, protect them with wire mesh from mice or birds that might take the seeds. A cold frame has an advantage in that the top can be used to stop heavy rain swamping the pots. But if the containers are stood in the shelter of a hedge or covered with an open-ended cloche they will survive well enough. Given this treatment such seeds usually germinate freely in spring. Even then alpine enthusiasts often keep the pots for a second or even third season before throwing out the contents. Some gentians, for example, may only appear sporadically over several springs.

It is worth giving this treatment to the seeds of any hardy plant that is a little out of the ordinary should it fail to germinate well from a spring sowing. Rather than throw them out, keep the pot outdoors over the following winter and see what happens. The value of this was well demonstrated to me some years ago when a pot of coloured cowslip seeds I had sown produced only two seedlings in the first spring, but more than two dozen appeared the following year after being chilled during the intervening winter.

Seeds needing to pass through a winter period before they germinate can often be fooled by being put in the cold part of a refrigerator (not the ice compartment) for a few weeks.

A point I must stress, however, is that cold alone is not enough to break the dormancy of some seeds. You can store such seeds in a refrigerator for years but it will not alter their inhibited germination one scrap. The seeds must also be moist as well, so it is sensible to sow them first.

But what if the seeds arrive too late for them to be conditioned naturally? To save wasting a complete season it is often possible to break their dormancy artificially in the following way. Sow the seeds in a container then slip it in the coldest part of a refrigerator - not the freezer compartment - for four to six weeks. At the end of this time move it to a shady cold frame and leave it to germinate naturally, doing nothing more than keeping the soil moist. Try to break their dormancy as early in the year as you can, however. If you bring seeds of plants from cold regions to germination point at midsummer, too high a temperature may then inhibit growth and frustrate, possibly ruin, your efforts.

True Stratification

This cold treatment given to break the dormancy of seeds, whether indoors or out, is called 'stratification'. The name derives from the old-established nursery practice of storing seeds between layers of moist sand for treatment, which was used especially for seeds in fleshy fruits like rose hips and haws. It is still a useful technique for a gardener, though on a much smaller scale, mixing the seeds or fruits with moist peat or sand in a polythene bag.

True stratification can be used to deal with seeds that have two inhibitors to germination, namely a water-impermeable coat and an embryo that remains dormant until chilled. Because cold itself cannot break dormancy, the seeds must first be induced to take up moisture. The type of seeds that behave this way are frequently those in berries and fruits that are normally eaten by birds - holly, yew and pyracantha, for example. The passage through the digestive system of the bird removes the water-proofing or sufficiently abrades the seed for water to penetrate, with the result that under natural conditions they germinate the following spring.

When such berries and fruits are gathered for their seeds, however, they miss out on this natural treatment, their seed coats remain impermeable and it can take 18 months in the soil for moisture to penetrate them. Even then they need a warm, followed by a cold period before they can grow. To save looking after a bare seedbed throughout this time the seeds can be stratified together for 6-18 months (depending on the type of plant) from the time they are gathered, then sown in the spring in which they are due to grow.

Ways have to be found to overcome the problem of water impermeability in some cases by soaking seeds in concentrated sulphuric acid for a limited time, while others respond to a wash in alcohol, but such methods are not practicable for home use. They have, however, led to one or two new items appearing in seed catalogues.

Two-stage Development

There are some plants where the germination is distinctly two-stage. Sown in the normal way the embryo responds, but only by producing a root underground. A cold period is then needed to break the dormancy of the shoot, so it is not until the second spring that you can see signs of growth. The tree paeony (*P. suffruticosa*) and some viburnums and yew behave in a strange way. So, too, do seeds of many lily species, including *Lilium auratum, L. monadelphum*, and *L. speciosum*, all of which only produce a small underground bulb in the first summer. These are obviously plants to sow in containers in a frame rather than in open ground where they could be swamped by weeds or accidentally hoed up.

A novel method suggested for lilies is to mix the seeds with moist peat in a screw-topped jar, arranging a few seeds close to the glass where you can see them, which can be kept in a warm airing cupboard for some 12 weeks. Keep an eye on the seeds by the glass and when the tiny bulbs have finished forming, gently tip them out and plant them in trays. If these are then kept at a temperature below 40F (4C), but not freezing, for a further 12 weeks their dormancy will be broken and they will grow normally.

Double Dormancy

Even stranger are the plants, mainly of the lily family, which have what is known as double dormancy. These are also two-stage developers, but both stages - first the root, then the shoot - need to have their dormancy broken in turn by a cold spell before they finally appear above soil. These therefore need to be sown in autumn and pass through the cold of two winters before you see signs of growth. Two wood lilies, *Trillium grandiflorum* and *T. erectum*, are examples of

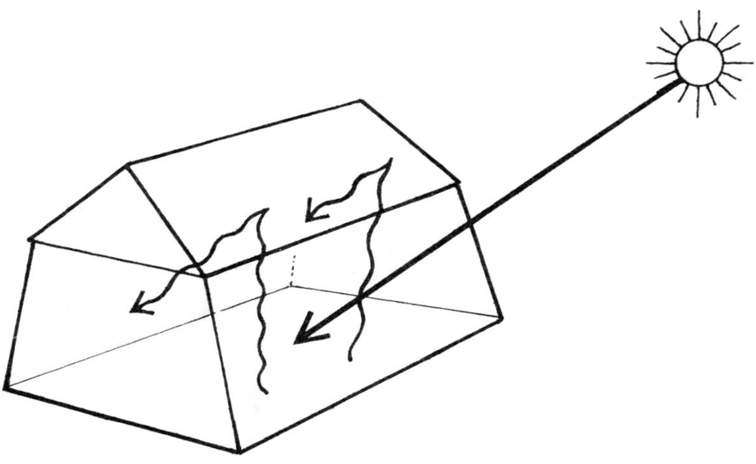

Glass is effective at trapping warmth because it allows penetration by the short wave energy from the sun, but reflects back long wave energy radiated from the soil and other objects.

dormancy also, although the right weather combination can provide sufficient stimulus for enough root growth in the first autumn to unbar the second stage, to allow the winter cold to break the dormancy of the shoot. Thus in some seasons it is possible for the double dormancy to be broken in a single autumn and winter if the seeds are sown early enough.

As you can see, raising natural plant species from seed, particularly those from areas where winters are long or cold, is not always quick or straight-forward. Indeed one is normally entering uncharted seas where little if anything is known about the majority, such as the optimum temperature requirements for germination. In such cases a gardener must rely almost entirely on his own knowledge and experience, coupled with some idea of the natural environment of such plants, to work out the best treatment. Patience is always an essential ingredient, of course, and mere forgetfulness is no substitute for it. At no stage should containers or seedbeds be allowed to dry out completely, but I shall have more to say on that point when we get down to practical details.

Catalogue Terms

Browsing through seed catalogues (see Appendix 7 - Sources of Supply) is a valuable and delightful occupation for anyone interested in raising his own plants. They often provide a lot of practical information as well as keeping one abreast of new developments. But they often contain one or two items that puzzle a newcomer to gardening, such as pelleted seeds. These are seeds that have been individually coated with a water-permeable substance to produce a more or less round pellet. The technique was originally devised to make it possible for commercial vegetable growers to sow awkward shaped seeds with a sophisticated seed drill that drops them at pre-determined intervals along the rows. This does away with the work of thinning out or singling the seedlings after they emerge. Chemicals to feed or protect the germinating seed and seedling can also be incorporated into the coating material. Pelleting is also sometimes used for very expensive flower seeds to allow them to be sown individually so that none is wasted.

Most seed firms offer pelleted seeds of a few varieties of plants, but I find many gardeners do not get very good germination from them. The problem is usually quite simple. The pellet has to absorb a fair amount of water before moisture reaches the seed and all too often the soil is just not wet enough. So far as home gardeners are concerned, unless they particularly wish to go in for critical spacing of seeds at sowing time, I do not believe pelleted seeds are worth the extra cost and certainly prefer to use ordinary seed myself. The possible exceptions are the very

There are two distinct ways in which plants develop at germination. In some cases the seed leaves (cotyledons) remain below ground, when the germination is said to be hypogeal (above). Usually, however, the seed leaves, which are easily distinguished from the 'true' leaves by their shape, are lifted into the air, when the germination is called epigeal (below). A common garden example of hypogeal germination is that of broad beans. Cabbages and lettuce demonstrate epigeal development.

expensive seeds like those of a few petunia varieties, which would be sown in boxes and kept well watered.

A large number of plants are described in seed catalogues as F1 hybrids. A hybrid is a cross between two species or different varieties of a plant. In the case of the F1 hybrids of catalogues, one specially produced group is used as mother plants to produce the seeds, another to provide only the pollen. In order to prevent any other plant getting into the act the work has to be isolated in some way, while the mother plants must also be prevented from pollinating each other. In some cases the work of pollination is done by hand. Producing such hybrids is an expensive business and that is why their seeds cost more to buy. But they offer particular advantages in their vigour and uniformity of development together with other special characteristics such as disease resistance perhaps, bigger flowers or, in the case of some vegetable crops, an ability to stand longer before spoiling or running to seed after they have reached maturity. For this reason they can be well worth the extra cost even if it doubles the price of a packet of seeds. There is no doubt that home gardeners have been able to grow far better crops of Brussels sprouts, for instance, by using F1 hybrid varieties, than they could before these were available.

If you do grow F1 hybrids do heed the seedsmen's warnings and do not try to save seed from them. Though they may have superb qualities these are not 'fixed' as they are in standard seed strains. Consequently their progeny are rarely as good and are frequently useless. The cost of producing F1 hybrids is very high also because the careful crossing of plants has to be done each time to produce a fresh batch of seed. The wholesale price of some F1 Begonia varieties, for instance, is approaching £4,000 per ounce (25 g) so you can understand why there may not be many seeds in a small packet.

One or two varieties of plants are offered as 'chitted seeds'. All this means is that the seeds have been brought to the stage where they have started to grow, which can sometimes be tricky. Once started, however, they can be planted carefully in pots and grown on in conditions normally suitable for that type of plant.

Perhaps I should also explain that 'seed potatoes' and 'seed shallots' are not seeds at all, but planting tubers and planting bulbs respectively. In both cases you have to use some part of the old plants to maintain a variety since they will not breed true to type from seed. It is possible to grow shallots from seed and they are quite acceptable. But in order to obtain seed at all you must use a strain that flowers easily, whereas what is normally wanted are non-flowering bulbs that will ripen and keep a long time.

Occasionally one finds a note in a catalogue or on a packet that the seeds have been 'dressed'. This term denotes that they have been treated with a special fungicide or insecticide. Regulations sometimes call for it when seed grown in one country is imported into another, to prevent the spread of pests or diseases into unaffected areas.

So much then for what seeds are, their basic needs and their odd habits. Armed with that knowledge we can go on to consider how best to prepare the soil and sow seeds in it to get consistently good results, beginning with sowings made in the open garden.

2. Sowing out of doors

Most of the plants we raise from seeds are sown out of doors in the open garden. The majority of vegetable crops are started that way, as are hardy annual flowers. Many hardy perennial plants and spring-flowering biennials are easily raised in an outdoor seedbed as well. Out of doors we rely on the weather over which we have no control, and the soil, that we can change to some extent to create the best conditions for seed germination and good growth. Since the soil plays such a vital part in gardening operations it is only sensible for gardeners to know what it is made of and how it behaves. Armed with that knowledge we can then use it and adapt it to our needs and, equally important, know how to look after it. For far from being the inert 'dirt' so many people imagine, fertile soil is teeming with life.

Types of soil

The major part of most soils is made up of particles of rock, ranging from stones through gravel, sand, silt to microscopic particles of clay. These give the mineral soils, as they are called, their basic textures and characteristics varying from the light, gritty, free-draining sandy soils to

Before sowing or planting in spring it is wise to test your soil to determine its plant food reserves and pH status.

the heavy, poorly drained clays. Most garden soils do not belong to one or other clearly defined type but are a mixture - what is termed a loam.

Even then it may favour one type or another and you could have a 'sandy loam' or a 'clay loam'. Where no one constituent predominates it would be a 'medium loam'- a term beloved by old garden writers and commonly met with in books - but a soil type that I've never been fortunate enough to find in my gardening career!

Because of their free-draining character, sandy and gravelly soils are less likely to become waterlogged in winter but tend to be hot and dry in summer. They can be worked easily throughout the year. Clay soils, on the other hand, stay wet and sticky in winter and are slow to dry out and warm up in spring. They can only be cultivated efficiently at those times when they are neither wet nor dry, but they are potentially richer in plant foods. The closer the soil is to a medium loam the less extreme is its behaviour.

Properties of Clay

Although the other particles are inert, those tiny particles of clay have colloidal properties, like gelatin, which enables them to swell and hold water when it is plentiful, yet shrink again as they lose it. This accounts for the way in which soils containing a lot of clay can shrink and crack

A pH test meter gives a reading in seconds to assess whether a plot of soil would benefit from liming.

badly in dry weather. It also explains why clay is sticky when wet and can be so difficult to remove from your tools and boots. Clay is also able to hold plant foods in the soil by chemical means to prevent them from being leached out in wet weather.

The basic rock from which the soil was derived also affects its chemical nature. Where there is chalk or limestone present the ground is alkaline in reaction. In other areas it can vary from neutral to acid: even very acid in some cases. Acidity or alkalinity are measured on what is called the pH scale and you can buy a simple, inexpensive soil-test kit or electronic meter to determine the pH status of your own soil. This information is essential because not only does the behaviour of a soil vary to some extent according to its pH, but there are many plants that will only survive where the soil is acid. Typical examples are rhododendrons, azaleas, as well as most heathers and some gentians, which object to chalk or lime in any form and quickly look sick if they are affected by it.

Need for Humus

The second major constituent of fertile soil is humus. This is a dark, amorphous substance formed by the break-down of organic matter, whether of animal or vegetable origin. Leaves, stems, roots and other plant debris, as well as wool, feathers, animal droppings, dead insects...all eventually contribute to the soil's stock of humus. Humus replacement is a continuous natural process under normal conditions.

Humus is vital for its effect on the soil as a conditioner. It is another 'colloid' and thus capable of holding moisture and food in the upper layers where plant roots can get at them, which is of special benefit to light, sandy soils. It also causes mineral particles to bind together to form groups or crumbs which improve the aeration and drainage of heavy soils. Being dark coloured itself, humus also darkens the soil. And because dark-coloured objects absorb the sun's warmth more quickly than light-coloured ones, which tend to reflect it, a soil well supplied with humus can reach a germinating temperature more quickly in the spring.

A teeming population of soil organisms is the third constituent of fertile soil. Some, like earthworms, are large enough to be seen, but the vast majority of them are microscopic. There can be millions of them in a teaspoonful (5 ml) of fertile soil. The larger part of this population of organisms is the workforce responsible for the conversion of raw organic matter into humus, in the process of which plant foods are released. Eventually, however, the humus is oxidised as well. A regular supply of bulky organic matter, together with a supply of air and moisture, is needed to maintain this thriving community. A certain amount of calcium (lime) is also needed to neutralise the acid by-products of decomposition. If lime is not present the soil becomes so acid that the whole process of converting organic matter into humus is slowed down. Peaty soils were formed almost entirely from partially decomposed organic matter where lack of air due to waterlogging and excessive acidity prevented further breakdown by the normal agents of decay.

Moisture and Air

An adequate supply of moisture and air must be held in the soil to trigger the germination of seeds and support the subsequent growth of the plants. Apart from the water held in colloidal particles, the rest of it is present as a film around each particle and especially where they touch each other. The larger spaces between the particles or clusters of particles is filled with air. The size of the particles therefore controls how much air and water can be held naturally by any mineral soil. The smaller the particle size the greater is their combined surface area in a cubic inch of soil. You can see this must be so if you consider a 1 in (2 cm) cube. If you divide it vertically through th centre to make two equal-sized pieces, each would have a new 1 sq in (2 sq cm) face. The surface area of the pieces would therefore be 2 sq in (5 sq cm) greater than that of the original cube. The more times you divide the cube, the greater the total surface area of the pieces would be and the more water they could hold in a surface film.

The smaller the particles, however, the closer they pack together and less room there is for air. If you look at a dish of apples you can clearly see the spaces between them, but not between particles of sugar in a bowl. Although this scale is larger, the effect is much the same between different sized soil particles. A cubic foot (30 cubic cm) of clay soil is much heavier than a sandy one because it contains a greater volume of rock mineral and water and less air.

Water is essential to green plants for three prime reasons. They use it to keep their soft cells turgid. It is also a raw material which they use in the process of photosynthesis by which they manufacture carbohydrates in their leaves. Water is also the medium in which plants absorb the mineral foods they need from the soil in the form of dissolved salts. But soil air is equally vital to a plant's welfare since it respires, or breathes, through the surface of its roots as well as its leaves. This is an important factor for gardeners to appreciate and soil management must be concerned with maintaining a balance between the two.

The only way for air to enter the soil is through the surface and the

Lime is best applied over the roughly dug soil in winter and left for the rains to wash in.

concentration of carbon dioxide increases, while that of oxygen lessens, the deeper you go. This is due to the respiration of plant roots and soil organisms. The oxygen is replenished by a process of diffusion, not a complete change of air. Anything which slows this down can retard the development of plants and slow the work of beneficial organisms. If air is completely excluded for any length of time by waterlogging, where water fills the air spaces, suffocation results. On the other hand, too well aerated a soil dries out too quickly and becomes too hot in summer, while the loss of its humus content can be accelerated.

Plant Foods

Plants need to take up a wide variety of substances from the soil in order to grow. Some, like iron and boron, they need in very tiny amounts and these are known as 'trace elements' (see page 10). Others they need in quite large quantities and include sulphur, calcium, nitrogen, phosphorus and potassium. It is the last three, however, which are generally in short supply, though liming the soil to provide calcium can be important in some areas and for some crops.

Nitrogen (N), phosphorus (P) or phosphates, and potassium (K), or potash as gardeners usually refer to it, are mainly derived from the breakdown of bulky organic manures. Even then the amount available is often rarely enough to provide bumper crops of vegetables and many flowers and fruits. But the supply can be augmented with the use of fertilisers, which supply them in concentrated form. Such fertilisers can be of organic origin - bone meal or hoof and horn meal for example - or manufactured chemically, like sulphate of ammonia. They can supply a single food, either N, P or K, or a balanced amount of all three. Somewhere on the container it will state the percentage of

N, P and or K the fertiliser provides. Being concentrated, however, fertilisers must be used with care. It is all too easy to overdose to the point where they become harmful. Fertilisers provide little or no humus and are therefore not a substitute for organic manure, but properly used together, each can enhance the result of the other.

Under natural conditions a cycle develops where plants grow, shed their leaves and eventually die. What they take out of the soil is mostly returned to it either in the form of leaves or other plant remains or the droppings of herbivorous animals that graze on them. In a cultivated garden, this is not the case. We take the vegetables and fruit produced for our own use and remove much of the natural debris from ornamental areas in the process of tidying up. Consequently garden soils tend to lack humus and plant foods, their structure deteriorates under cultivation and their moisture-holding capacity and aeration become seriously impaired. The basis of good soil management therefore is the maintenance and, better still, improvement of its humus content. Humus is the ingredient that can affect the disadvantages inherent in any extreme type of mineral soil, be it too heavy or too light.

How Humus Works

Many people find it difficult to understand how humus can improve both the moisture-holding capacity of sandy soils and the drainage of heavy ones. Such seemingly conflicting effects are due to the fact that humus is capable both of holding water itself like a sponge and of binding the soil particles together into groups to form crumbs. More moisture can be held within a tight group than could be held around the individual particles that go to make it. But the crumbs do not pack so closely together and so there are larger pore spaces between them to allow excess moisture to drain through to the lower levels and let air penetrate more freely.

To provide the necessary humus, land which is regularly tilled should have bulky organic matter dug into it at least every third year. It can be in the form of stable or farmyard manure, garden compost (made by rotting down weeds, leaves, straw and other plant debris) or old mushroom compost, and should be used at rates of about 1 cwt (51 kg) to 6-8 sq yd (6-8 sq m). The actual amount of humus derived from a ton of manure is very little but since it is extremely powerful in its action it has a potent effect.

It can be more convenient in a town to buy a proprietary brand of concentrated manure by the plastic sackful. This has been pre-rotted by composting to reduce the bulk. Consequently a much smaller

Adding bulk organic matter when digging is an important part of soil management. It is needed to maintain the humus content that is essential to a good soil structure.

A dressing of peat worked into the surface can be of great benefit when preparing difficult ground for sowing. It helps to separate the particles of sticky soils and to prevent a surface crust from forming.

volume is needed, compared with raw manure, to produce the equivalent amount of humus. Although more expensive to buy, it is easier to handle, less bulky to store, and unlikely to upset the neighbours as a smelly load of ripe manure can do. Equally useful producers of humus are peat and composted bark. Both are clean to handle but are relatively expensive to use on a large scale and provide only negligible amounts of plant food.

Fresh, raw manure should be dug into the soil during autumn or winter to give time for the organisms to get to work on it before crops are grown on the ground. Old manure that has been stacked for at least six months and preferably a year, concentrated manure, peat,

Where the soil is really clayey it pays to mix in a heavy dressing of peat and gritty sand to an area to create a permanent bed specially for plant raising.

composted bark, mushroom manure and well-made garden compost can be mixed with the soil at any time.

Other Soil Conditioners

Apart from humus, there are two other important soil conditioners that help in the formation of a good crumb structure on clay soils - frost and lime. Particles of clay are flat and plate-like. They tend to pack down flat and, when moist, stick tenaciously together like sheets of wet glass. In winter, however, the moisture expands on freezing to force the particles apart and upset their alignment. Then, when the soil surface dries out in spring it is easy to create the fine surface tilth necessary for seed sowing and germination.

To gain maximum benefit from winter weathering, all ground containing clay should be turned over in rough lumps in autumn and winter. This speeds drainage and allows the frost to strike as deeply as possible to shatter the clods and leave the soil loose. Such winter digging of vacant ground is best completed by the end of December if possible.

Lime can be an important conditioner of acid clay soils since it, too, can cause the particles to group together into crumbs. The best form to use for this purpose is hydrated lime, which is a very fine powder. It is best applied to the rough dug soil in winter and left for the rain to wash in. Spread it over the soil immediately it is dug if no manure was added. Where manure is buried, wait until February before applying the lime, because the calcium in the lime will speed the release of plant foods from the manure which could then be washed away before plants have time to absorb them.

Lime should never be added as a matter of course, but only if a soil test (see page 22) shows the soil to be really acid, and then only give enough lime to make it moderately acid. An overdose will make the soil alkaline, which could cause problems, such as making the iron content unavailable to plants. Because so many ornamental plants become sick if there is free lime in the soil, liming is usually confined to vegetable plots. Only if the soil is so acid that it prevents proper plant growth would it be used in other parts of the garden. Although it is simple enough to make an acid soil alkaline, it is by no means easy to reverse the process and make alkaline soil acid.

Having created a good soil crumb structure, with all the benefits of good moisture-holding ability combined with aeration and drainage, it is important to take care not to destroy it again by working or walking on the soil while it is too wet. For once it is broken down it may take another winter to build it up again. Heavy, sticky soils are the most difficult to handle and need special care. Never try to work them when they are wet enough to stick badly to your tools and boots. It also pays to stand on boards while you work, especially once a surface tilth has been prepared for sowing, to preserve its texture.

When to Start Sowing

Spring is the most important time for sowing seeds out of doors. That is the time when many vegetable crops are sown as well as seeds of hardy annual flowers and many perennial plants. The work begins in March or April, according to the season, where you live and the soil type. You cannot go by the calendar, however, but only by the state of the soil, which must have dried out sufficiently to allow you to work it and create a seedbed. By then it should have warmed up sufficiently to encourage the germination of hardy plants.

When we are lucky enough to have a week of drying winds in March, the ground often becomes dry enough to get in the first sowings of vegetables early. But the period when the soil is fit to work is often no more than a day or two before the weather becomes wet again at that time of year. You must grasp the opportunity quickly if you want to grow really early outdoor crops. In other seasons April may be the earliest time one can make a start.

The odd weed seedling popping up here and there is a sure sign that the soil is warm enough for sowing. And people who live in rural areas are usually in no doubt when soil is fit to work due to the frantic burst of activity in the fields as farmers set about their spring sowings. The chief sign to look for in your own garden is a drying out of the soil surface. Once you can work the ground without having to continually clean soil from the teeth of your rake it is time to begin.

Do not become over anxious to get started however. Nothing is to be gained by sowing seeds in cold, soggy, ill-prepared ground. To do so is to invite germination failures and any seedlings which do appear are usually sickly. A batch sown later, when conditions are right, can make far better plants, even out-stripping the earlier sowings in development and cropping power. Always be guided by the state of the soil, therefore, and not by the date in spring.

Preparing the Ground

The ideal seedbed consists of a firm, flat area of ground covered with an inch or two (2-5 cm) of finely broken down soil - the tilth - that is free of large stones, twigs or other debris. It takes time and effort to prepare, but repays the effort spent on it. The most difficult part of preparing a good seed bed is creating this surface tilth, but it is vital for small seeds. A good tilth enables you to make seed drills - shallow furrows - easily to an even depth, which allows all the seedlings to appear at more or less the same time. It also means there are no holes or cracks in the base of the drill for the seeds to fall down where they might be too deep to germinate. When the seeds are covered over the fineness of the soil ensures they are surrounded and in intimate contact with it and so able to absorb the moisture they need. And by removing stones and debris you make sure there is nothing to impede the seedlings from pushing through the soil covering into the light.

As it dries out in spring, a plot that was dug before Christmas should be in an ideal state, with the top few inches fine and friable and any remaining lumps at or near the surface ready to crumble if knocked with a tool or kicked with your foot. Provided the ground is reasonably level, without huge peaks and valleys due to the soil being thrown up unevenly during the digging, you can make a start by

Spread any fertiliser required evenly over the area. Keep your hand close to the ground if the weather is windy.

applying a base dressing of any fertiliser you may wish to use, scattering it evenly over the whole area. If the soil surface is uneven, however, this should be roughly levelled first or you may move the fertiliser in the process so that some parts are overdosed, while other areas receive little or none.

The best fertiliser for the average gardener to use is a general, balanced one that contains nitrogen, phosphates and potash in roughly the same proportions. A typical one is that called Growmore, with an analysis of 7N: 7P: 7K, but there are plenty more on the market made from organic or inorganic ingredients which are similar. The ideal would be to test the soil first to see what food is available then add a specially compounded mixture to balance the food reserves to suit the plants that will grow there. While this may pay dividends where a lot of one type of plant is to be grown, under ordinary garden conditions the number and diversity of plants put in is so great that a general fertiliser is usually the best compromise. It would be difficult, to say the least, to attempt to meet the exact requirements of every plant!

Tread and Rake

Having spread the fertiliser, follow this up by treading. This is done by shuffling up and down over the area, keeping your feet close

Mix the fertiliser into the soil surface with the aid of a fork, breaking down large clods as you work.

Shuffle up and down over the plot to firm it. This will also help by crushing small lumps.

together and with your weight on your heels, in such a way that each line of footprints falls adjacent to the one before. The object of treading is twofold. It firms the soil to make it more suitable for plant roots and prevent it drying out quickly. In the process lumps are crushed by your weight. It is a fallacy to believe that plants like to grow in soft, loose soil: they do not. They are adapted to have their roots in intimate contact with firm soil. Indeed this is essential not only to assist their water absorption, but also to give them stability and prevent their roots being wrenched and damaged, as well as to keep the plants standing upright.

Treading is followed by raking to create a finely broken down surface layer 1-2 in (2-5 cm) deep. Raking can be a tedious business, particularly on unweathered clay soil, but the production of a good surface tilth is essential if seedlings are going to have the best chance. Even when such raking is time-consuming, however, you can take consolation in the fact that it can make the work of thinning, weeding and hoeing much easier later on.

In the process of raking the soil is loosened to the depth required, lumps crushed and any stones, pieces of root or other rubbish combed out. When finished there should be an even depth of loose fine soil over the whole area. Also leave the surface as flat as possible to prevent any possibility of puddles forming in a wet spell.

Finally rake the area thoroughly to create a 1-2 inch (2-5 cm) surface layer of finely crumbled soil - the tilth.

It may be necessary to tread and rake a plot more than once to break down all the surface lumps, especially when it is dry. But beware of over-treading a heavy soil even if it is dry on the surface, because it is still possible to over-compact it lower down. For this reason clay soil is best trodden no more than once in springtime, especially if it is lacking humus.

Moisten Dry Ground

When ground to be prepared for sowing has just been cleared of a crop, either in late spring, or summer, it should first be dug with a fork and broken up as finely as possible. A small mechanical cultivator can be used to do the job much more quickly. Whether doing the work by hand or with a machine, if the ground is bone dry, it pays to water the area thoroughly a day or two in advance to soften it. This is best done using a sprinkler that creates a fine mist that penetrates gently yet deeply without ruining the soil texture.

Where the ground is moist and sticky in spring it can help enormously if a layer of fine peat is raked into the soil surface when preparing it for sowing. This is also a worthwhile practice on any soil that tends to form a surface crust after rain. The peat ensures the surface remains moist for a longer period as well as helping to keep it open.

Really heavy clay soils can be heartbreaking if not winter dug or if their texture is spoiled. When wet the soil is too sticky to rake; when dry the lumps become flint hard and defy anything less than the blow of a hammer to break them. Only when they are drying out after being wetted can such lumps be broken down with a rake. This means catching the soil just at the right stage after a shower of rain, though on a small scale you can apply sufficient water with a rosed can, working over a square yard (square metre) at a time, to do the trick.

The best answer on such ground is to prepare a special area as a permanent seedbed to use to raise plants, for transplanting. Over a small area it is possible to change the soil texture by adding coarse sand or grit as well as garden compost or peat. Clay burnt on a bonfire loses its stickiness for ever and breaks down like brick dust. This, together with charcoal debris from a wood fire, can also be used to help lighten an area of heavy ground. I must warn you however, that it takes a 6 in (15 cm) layer of sand intimately mixed with the top 8-10 in (20-25 cm) of soil to have much effect on clay. Furthermore, it must be coarse 'sharp sand' - not soft, builders' sand. Though an expensive, not to say laborious job to obtain and mix in so much sand, the result is extremely long lasting.

Having prepared the ground it saves time to make all the rows of a seed bed before you begin sowing.

Sowing the Seeds

Once the work of preparing the soil is completed, that of actually sowing the seeds is not at all laborious. The most common method of sowing most seeds out of doors is to sow them in shallow drills or furrows. To ensure the drills are straight and correctly spaced, use a garden line pulled really taut as a guide. Make the drills by pulling the corner of a draw hoe through the soil while keeping the blade against the line. Keeping one foot on the line while you work prevents the hoe pushing it out of place. At the same time take care to make the drill of even depth along its whole length. This ensures that all the seedlings appear at about the same time.

The depth of sowing depends, of course, on the seeds being dealt with, some needing to be sown deeper than others. The majority are happy when covered with about ½ in (1 cm) of soil, but the depth to sow is usually included in the instructions on most seed packets. Some of the smaller flower seeds, however, need only ⅛-¼ in (3-5 mm) of soil above them. Drawing out drills for these is difficult since a hoe tends to dig in too deeply. Here the best answer is to use a pointed piece of wood instead, or even press a broom handle or the edge of a

Having run out a sufficient length of garden line, hook it under the lower horn to prevent it unreeling any further.

Pull the line taut and push the reel spike in at a backward angle to further tighten the line and prevent it slipping from under the lower horn.

board into the soil surface to make a suitable indentation.

All seeds need adequate moisture to trigger their germination. If the soil seems rather dry when you make a drill, or if it is sandy and likely to dry out quickly and the weather seems 'set fair', flood the drill with water immediately before sowing. Just walk along the row allowing water to dribble out of the spout of a can straight into the drill. It takes about a gallon (4.5 litres) to thoroughly moisten a 20 ft (6 m) row.

Having opened a drill and ensured it is moist, the next stage is to sow the seeds very thinly along it. Most home gardeners tend to sow the seeds far too thickly, with the result that the seedlings compete with one another as soon as they germinate. Generally there is little point in sowing more than 2-4 seeds per inch (2 cm) of row. Then, allowing for the fact that not all the seeds will grow and that a few will succumb to pests or diseases, you should still have an adequate stand of seedlings for most purposes. In the case of seeds large enough to handle easily, two or three can be sown wherever a plant is required to grow rather than scatter them along the whole line, but it does add to the time taken.

Handling Technique

Handling small seeds can be difficult until you get the knack. The best way is to take a large pinch between two fingers and thumb and

Preparing for Spring Sowing
Sowing Technique
Draw shallow seed drills with the corner of a hoe. Put one foot on the line to help keep it straight.

Whenever the soil seems to be rather dry, flooding the drills with water immediately before sowing will encourage quick and even germination.

gradually release them while moving your hand along above the drill. You will find this can be done by gradually sliding your thumb across

After scattering the seeds thinly yet evenly along the whole length of the drill.

Draw the loosened soil back into the furrow with your rake to cover the seeds.

the finger tips. Round seeds like those of cabbages and turnips are the easiest to handle. The more pointed their shape, however, the more difficult it becomes. Alternatively you can buy one of the plastic seed 'sowers' that are adjustable according to the seed size and which release them in a trickle. Beware of sowing seeds by shaking them straight out of the packet - it is too easy to accidentally tip out too

Then tamp it down along the row to make it firm and cut surface evaporation.

An alternative method of closing the seed drills is to shuffle along the row in such a way that your feet push the loose soil back into the furrow and your heels compress it.

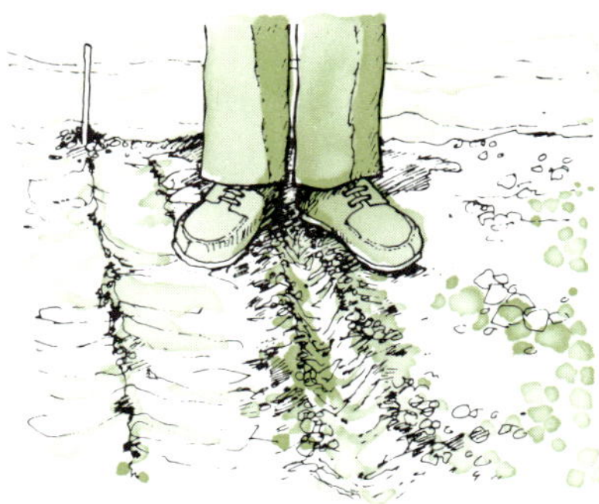

many, or even have them blow away in a strong wind.

Finally comes the job of covering the seeds with soil and firming it over them. One method is to draw the excavated soil back into the drill with the aid of a rake, then tamp it down along the row, using the head of the rake by holding the handle upright. This is the only sensible method to use where you are trying not to walk on and over-compress the soil.

On sandy soil and other ground when it is not too wet the whole operation can be done with your feet. With a foot on either side of the row shuffle slowly forwards along it keeping your heels together and toes apart. Your boots will funnel the loose soil into the drill and your heels then compress it.

Firming is Essential

The need to firm the covering soil over the seeds cannot be over emphasised. By pressing the seeds into close contact with the soil it ensures they can absorb the moisture needed as quickly as possible. It also lessens the chance of the soil drying out due to excessive evaporation before germination occurs. Equally important in the case of some seeds is the need to keep the seed case firmly anchored in the soil so that it is not dragged out by the developing seedling. Typical examples are onions and leeks - these are looped over like staples when they first appear, the tip of the seed leaf continuing to draw food from the seed in the soil even after emergence. If the soil is not made really firm at sowing time, the seed case is dragged out to sit on top of the seedling like a black cap. Another common example is the marrow family, whose seedlings can apppear with the old seed case clipping the seed leaves together which prevent proper development.

The position of each row should be indicated by pushing a stick in at either end of it. There will be nothing else to show you where it is until the seedlings appear, which can take up to six weeks in some cases. I find it a great help to scatter a little radish seed along the rows of such slow-germinating plants as parsley and parsnips before filling in the drills. The radish come up quickly and serve to mark the rows so that you can hoe between them to keep down weeds before the main plants put in an appearance. The radishes must be sown very thinly, dropping the seeds 6-8 in (15-20 cm) apart. Sown closer together there is a danger that they will spoil the other seedlings by smothering them when they eventually do appear.

Label Your Sowings Clearly

As each type of seed is sown, label the rows clearly. Write the sowing date as well as the name of the plant on the label. I find it useful, too, to include any other information I may need to know later - such as the plant height, flower colour and distance apart to which the seedlings should be thinned. It is an advantage, when sowing a

Make a point of labelling your rows as they are sown. It is all too easy to get into a muddle later, especially when sowing different varieties of the same plant.

number of different kinds of seed, to write the labels out beforehand when you can do it in comfort, sitting at a table.

There is no need to draw drills for the seeds which are large enough to be handled individually, like those of beans, marrows and sweet corn. These can be sown where plants are required to grow, making a hole with a trowel and sowing two seeds about 1 in (2 cm) apart at each station. Where seedlings appear in pairs, the weaker one can be pulled up. I find this a better method than sowing the seeds singly and putting in a few extra ones at the end of a row to provide spare plants to transplant into any gaps where a seedling fails to emerge. There is usually ample seed in a packet for double sowing, while transplanted seedlings so often lag behind the rest.

A useful, labour-saving method for controlling weeds is to cover the soil with black polythene sheeting, which effectively smothers any weed that tries to grow under it. Though normally only used where young plants are set out, such a plastic mulch can be put down before putting seeds of plants that can be sown individually where they are to grow. Having prepared the area for sowing, the plastic sheeting is spread over the soil and its edges buried to hold it in place. This is best done by trapping them in slits made in the ground with the aid of a spade which are then trodden shut again. Holes for the seeds are easily punched through the plastic with a trowel or dibber when sowing them. To prevent the plastic balooning up in windy weather it is sometimes necessary to weigh it down with stones or a few spadefuls of soil scattered on top.

Apart from smothering weeds a black plastic mulch is extremely efficient at warming the soil as well. It is therefore invaluable for

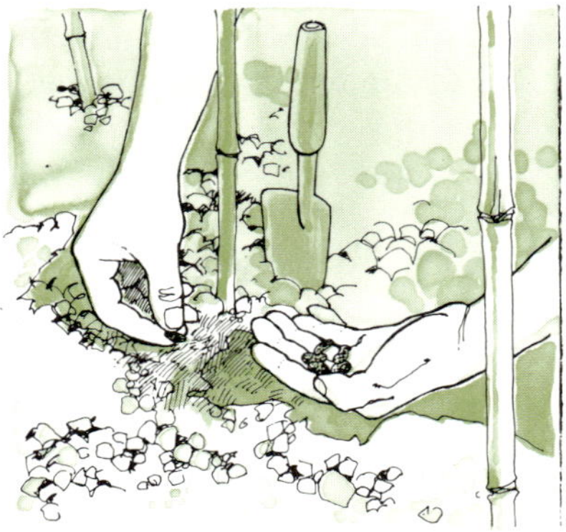

Sow runner beans in pairs at the base of each stake or cane and press the soil firm on top of them. Later remove the weaker seedling if both grow.

Sow the flat seeds of marrows and cucumbers on edge, setting two or three an inch or so apart wherever you want a plant to grow.

speeding the growth for such crops as early broad beans and the tender sweet corn, courgettes and marrows, that do so much better when their roots are really warm.

As when using any mulch, you must ensure that the soil is moist before you put the plastic in place. Also scatter slug bait over the soil as well, if these are a problem pest in your garden. The disadvantages of a plastic mulch are the fiddle of putting it in place and its appearance, which can be off-putting. But these are a small price to pay for the labour it can save, especially if you are using an old neglected garden or allotment where the soil has become liberally endowed with weed seeds.

The usual method of sowing peas is to draw out a wide drill, using the full width of a hoe blade or shovelling out the soil with a spade, then sowing three staggered rows of seeds along the bottom of it. I find it far quicker and just as effective to draw two narrow drills 6 in (15 cm) apart and sow the seeds along them. This also enables you to run a narrow hoe between the rows once or twice before supports are needed, which saves a lot of time hand weeding later.

Where possible, rows of plants should be arranged to run north to south. Sited in this way each side of the row has a chance of receiving the same amount of sunlight.

Bands and Patches

The advantages of sowing seeds in lines is chiefly one of convenience. It enables you to hoe between rows to save a lot of hand weeding and gives space for your feet when moving among and tending the plants. But it is not always the best way to utilise an area if you have only a small plot since, in some instances, you can get bigger crops and raise more plants by growing them in wide bands or patches. Vegetables worth growing in this way include carrots, beetroot, radish and small upright lettuces, like the variety called Little Gem. It can also save space to grow in the same way seedlings of plants that are to be transplanted later, be they vegetables or flowers. In fact, anything that needs only a few inches of space until it is transplanted or harvested does not need to be grown in rows spaced 10-12 in (25-30 cm) apart.

Measure a strip of bed about 4 ft (120 cm) wide, which will allow you to reach to the centre from either side. The seed can be scattered over the surface and worked in with the aid of a rake or sown in a series of closely set rows.

While such a system can make much better use of space there are two essential points you must always remember. Firstly, being closer together the plants will require a larger amount of food and water from each square foot (30 sq cm) of soil. Secondly it will involve you in a lot of time-consuming thinning and weeding by hand, since there will not be room to use a hoe. Nonetheless it is a technique that can be of great help to anyone whose gardening scope is limited by an acute lack of space.

Making a Seedbed for Transplanting

When raising seedlings of vegetables or flowers that are later to be transplanted elsewhere it is sensible to group them together in a seedbed where they can be looked after. This need not be very large and a piece of ground wide enough to give 3 ft (90 cm) long drills is ample for the average gardener who does not need more than a dozen or so plants of any kind. The rows can be set quite close together, but it is wise to leave enough space to be able to hoe easily if you do not want a lot of hand weeding to do.

Having prepared the area for sowing, thrust short canes into the soil to mark where each end of the rows will be. Those thin, green, split canes sold in garden shops and centres quite cheaply by the hundred are ideal for the purpose. A short length of board placed against each pair of canes in turn makes a good guide when making the drills and saves fiddling about with a line. You will find, too, that the short-handled onion hoe (see page 108) or pointed piece of wood is more convenient for the purpose than an ordinary hoe, which is too long and unwieldy. Put one foot on the board to hold it steady as you work. As with making other sowings, remember to flood the drills

Wherever possible always work from a path or board in spring, especially if the soil is heavy to avoid over compressing it and spoiling its texture.

with water before sowing if the soil is on the dry side and firm the soil over the seeds when the drills are covered in again.

Such a seedbed is ideal for raising brassica seedlings, many hardy plants and biennial flowers also, if you do not need too large a quantity. Where many plants of one kind are required it is better to find space in the vegetable plot for one or more long rows.

Early Sowing Tips

Of all sowings made out of doors it is those of the earliest vegetables that usually seem to give most disappointment to gardeners. While you can wait until mid-April or even May before putting in seeds of annual and perennial plants and the main vegetable crops, those first vegetable sowings, hopefully made in March, are vital if you are to enjoy the earliest pickings. Failures are more often due to faulty technique than to the seeds.

To begin with, as already explained, the soil must be in a fit condition to work in order to create the necessary 'tilth'. It is essential to dig heavy ground *before* Christmas if you want to make a really early start.

Owing to the lower soil temperature, early sowings are always slow to develop at first. To ward off attacks of soil pests and diseases it pays where possible to treat the seeds with a special seed dressing. This is a powder containing both fungicide and insecticide. You simply put a little into an open seed packet, then close the end and shake it so that all the seeds become coated with the powder. It is a quick and cheap way of helping to avoid germination failures due to underground attack and is especially valuable with early sowings that tend to hang fire.

Cloches Boost Growth

A way of gaining a head start with outdoor sowings is the use of cloches. These portable covers of plastic or glass are put in position 2-4 weeks beforehand, to dry out and warm up the soil. Fork over and roughly level the soil first, then put down a line as a guide to keep the cloches straight. Butt them close together and close up the ends of the

To get full value from cloches they need to be kept in use. But try to arrange matters so that they are simply moved from one row to the next and do not have to be carted around the garden.

rows. As soon as the soil can be raked, choose a dry day to remove the cloches to one side, fertilise, tread and rake the ground, sow the seeds and put the cloches back into place. Cloches come in many shapes and sizes and the space allowed between the rows of seeds should be adjusted in order to fit the maximum number under the cloches and so make the best use of them.

All the crops normally sown out of doors in March should conditions be suitable, can be sown under cloches in February. Even March sowings can gain a fortnight over unprotected outdoor sowings if covered by cloches. These not only provide extra warmth but prevent rain from battering the soil surface and are especially valuable where the soil tends to form a hard crust as it dries out. There is no need to keep the cloches over early sowings until they reach maturity. Instead, move them in late April to a fresh site where they can be used to forward extra early sowings of such tender crops as marrows, sweet corn and dwarf beans. Cloches are not confined to vegetable production of course, but can also be used to raise an early batch of hardy annuals, protect sowings of hardy plants or to raise half-hardy annuals such as zinnias and China asters sown in open ground where they are to flower (see Appendix 3).

It is the protection they provide from cold winds and rain as much as the trapping of warmth that makes cloches so effective early in the year. As the season progresses they should have gaps left between them for ventilation. And in high summer they may need to have a liquid greenhouse shading material sprayed or painted on them to prevent tender leaves and shoots being scorched in intense sunlight. At other times they are best kept spotlessly clean to ensure the plants under them benifit from as much light as possible, especially in the spring and autumn. To save time and effort, try to arrange your cropping plans so that cloches can be moved to an adjacent strip each time, rather than have to be carried from one part of the garden to another.

Fluid Sowing

Another way of speeding early sowings is by the technique called 'fluid sowing'. The seeds are kept warm and moist indoors until they begin to sprout. Then they are stirred into a carrier jelly. This mixture is then put into a plastic bag with a corner cut off and squeezed out along the seed drill, rather in the manner a cook squeezes icing from a bag when decorating cakes, and covered in the usual way. It results in quicker emergence and a better stand of seedlings.

It is possible to buy a fluid sowing kit from some seed firms and garden centres. Or you can make use of home equipment. The seeds

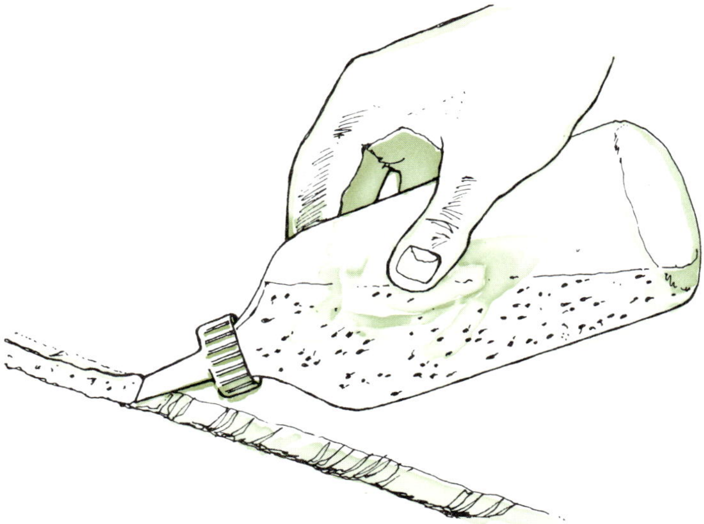

Use of a special plastic dispenser makes it a quick and easy job to sow the mixture of 'jelly' and seeds along the drills.

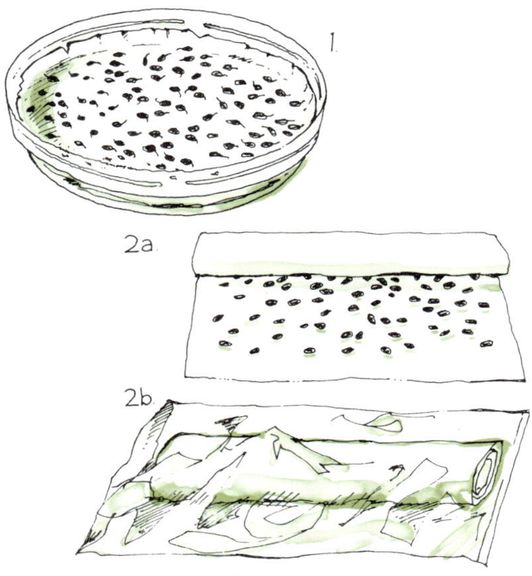

Seeds are sprouted indoors by spreading them thinly over absorbent paper that is kept moist in a closed plastic container (1). They take up less space if scattered over moist kitchen paper towelling then carefully rolled up (2a) and slipped into a clean polythene bag (2b) until they begin to shoot. In either case keep them in a warm place, make sure they do not dry out and examine them regularly. Once the seeds show signs of sprouting, move them into a refrigerator if you cannot sow them at once.

can be sprouted on moist paper kitchen towel over a thick layer of tissues in a plastic sandwich box with a snap-on lid. When they are ready wash the seeds out into a fine sieve, then stir them into the 'jelly', for which a fungicide-free, cellulose-based paste intended for wallpaper can be used. Some seeds sprout very quickly so you must look at them twice a day. Should they be ready before you can sow them, they can be stored unfrozen in a refrigerator for a while.

Time to Stop

The main season for making sowings out of doors usually comes to an end about the first or second week of July. This is the time when, over most of the southern half of Britain at least, final batches of summer lettuce, beetroot and other crops are put in to provide late season supplies. Sown any later they are unlikely to have time to mature. Here again, cloches can make a huge difference. Where crops can be covered in September, to speed their development in the shorter colder days of autumn, final sowings of summer crops can be delayed until August (see Appendix 4).

The last major outdoor sowings of all are of those plants that are to stand over winter as seedlings to provide a specially early harvest the following spring. They include August-sown onions, both Japanese bulbing and salad kinds, spring cabbages, September-sown winter lettuce and November-sown round-seeded peas and broad beans. Many hardy annuals can also be sown in late summer and the seedlings overwintered when they not only flower earlier than those sown in spring, but make much larger plants.

To make a success of these late sowings you must choose suitable varieties. Not all have the same winter hardiness. The ground too, must be well drained and protected from freezing north and east winds. Few gardeners bother with these sowings apart from spring cabbages and, perhaps, the special Japanese onions. But once again cloches can make an enormous difference to the survival rate of seedlings, particularly in a harsh winter, so much so that they really are worth attempting in most gardens if you have cloches available to cover the rows during the worst of the winter.

Pest Control at Sowing Stage

Pest control is a necessary part of good husbandry and the chances of raising plants successfully from seed depend on your keeping pests at bay. That is not to say that you must perpetually wage war on pests, but know when to take sensible action against them. Garden pests come in many guises, but fortunately they do not all turn up every year and even then some of them only attack specific plants. They can be divided into two broad groups. First there are those that are dealt with if and when they put in an appearance. The others it is wise to guard against when you know the conditions will encourage them, either for the reason that they are certain to appear or because once entrenched there is little you can do to be rid of them.

Soil-inhabiting pests certainly come in the latter category, if only because you cannot see them or the damage they are doing until it is too late. And the time to set about controlling them is when making the seedbed or immediately the seeds are sown.

Wherever a new plot has been made from a piece of grassland, an old lawn, or reclaimed from a neglected weedy state, you are likely to have trouble with various cut worms, chafer grubs and leather jackets. These are larvae of various moths, beetles and craneflies. All will eat the roots or stems of plants at or below ground level. When you know you are likely to have trouble with them it pays to dress the area with a soil insecticide and work it into the surface when preparing it for sowing. Thereafter keep cultivated ground clear of grassy weeds that encourage these pests to lay eggs there.

Dealing with Rootflies

Cabbage rootfly is another pest to prevent if you can. It attacks cabbages, cauliflowers, Brussels sprouts and most other brassica crops. The flies lay their eggs beside the plants. When these hatch the larvae burrow down to begin feeding on the roots. Whenever you sow seeds or transplant seedlings of these plants the rows must be treated with a suitable soil insecticide to control this pest or you are almost certain to have trouble with stunted and dying plants later.

The same precautions must also be taken against carrot rootfly, the grubs of which will burrow into the roots of related parsley, parsnips and Hamburg parsley as well. I find it essential to treat rows of carrots at sowing time. For safety's sake I also treat parsley when sown, though the strength of the attacks against this and parsnips seems to vary from area to area of the country.

Although generally recommended to help control the above pests, the ordinary seed dressings you can buy just are not powerful enough used in the ordinary way. You can scatter the powder along the open drills as well, but it is cheaper and can be more effective in the long term to buy a proper soil insecticide to do the job.

3. Looking After the Seedlings

Merely getting good germination is only a part, though to many people the most difficult part, of raising plants from seed. From the moment the seeds appear above ground they are liable to be attacked by pests, while excessive competition from weeds or even overcrowding can quickly spoil them.

Weeds must be controlled for several reasons. Firstly many of them develop much more quickly than those of most garden plants. Consequently they can smother and spoil your seedlings by denying them the light and air needed to encourage sturdy growth. Less obvious, but equally important, is the fact that weeds also take up food and moisture from the soil that should be reserved for your plants. In some instances weeds can also harbour pests. Shepherd's purse, for instance, is a good host for flea beetles. Hoeing and hand weeding are the usual ways in which garden weeds are controlled among growing plants, though mulching - covering the soil with a layer of organic matter or black plastic - and chemical weedkillers can also be used in some circumstances.

Hoe Often

Hoeing is normally begun as soon as the rows of seedlings can be distinguished, using a Dutch hoe (see page 108). The blade is skimmed through the soil just below the surface to sever the weed seedlings. To be really successful this type of hoeing must be done while the seeds are still tiny. Once allowed to develop in size, many species, including groundsel, chickweed, buttercup and annual meadow grass, tend to root back into the soil except in very hot, dry weather. This is why it pays to sow a few radish seeds along the rows of slow-to-germinate plants. By coming up quickly, the radish mark the rows so that you can hoe between them before the weeds grow too large.

It is only the weed seeds in the surface layer of soil that will germinate, those further down lying dormant until future cultivation brings them to the surface. If you prepare your seedbed in advance, therefore, you can hoe off the first flush of weeds that develop even

Hoe between rows of young seedlings regularly. If weeds once get the upper hand they will quickly stifle and spoil your plants.

before sowing seeds of the plants you want to grow. For the same reason, the more often you hoe and the more weeds you destroy, the less there are to grow, provided you never allow weeds to develop and scatter seeds over the ground. If you can effectively hoe between seedlings three times over the first month, you should have very few weeds germinating to worry you thereafter. There are limits to how close you can hoe to seedlings, of course, so those in the rows or close to plants have to be removed by hand. So, too, do those that for one reason or another defy your attempts to kill them by hoeing!

Hoeing also has another advantage in that it keeps the soil surface loose. This can be of special benefit to seedlings where the soil tends to form a crust, or cap, after rain.

Stifle Weeds

Mulching is something that home gardeners rarely do, yet it can be a valuable technique. Such a covering tends to stifle weed seedlings that try to grow. It also helps to conserve soil moisture by cutting down surface evaporation. Equally important in some gardens is the fact that a mulch prevents the soil surface being beaten down by rain or drying to form a hard crust that can seriously impede the movement of air into the soil. Whatever the material used you should ensure that the soil is fully charged with moisture and weed free before applying the mulch. Also take care that organic mulches do not actually touch the bases of young plants.

Manure and garden compost are excellent mulching materials provided they are well rotted and not contaminated with a lot of weed seeds. Both can provide extra plant food that is washed into the ground by rain in wet periods, but not sufficiently rotted they may actually take nitrogen from the soil for a while, which can upset the growth of your plants. Peat and composted bark are also good for mulching, being clean and pleasant to handle. These provide no plant foods but are easily spread evenly around quite small plants and are, or should be, completely free of weed seed. Lawn mowings can also be used for mulching around larger plants provided they do not come from a weedy lawn or one recently dosed with a weedkiller. Do not spread them more than an inch (2 cm) deep, keep them away from the bases of the stems and be prepared to top-up the layer as it shrivels.

Black plastic sheeting is another good mulching material that I have already mentioned in the section dealing with sowing outdoors (page 39). Newspapers weighed down with stones or a little soil can also be surprisingly effective though very unsightly, but are worth considering where the soil is sandy and dries very quickly. Strips of old lino, wooden boards and large stones can all be pressed into use for the purpose. A layer of stone chippings or shingle is sometimes

Mulching - covering the surrounding soil - with a layer of organic matter helps keep the soil cool and moist around young plants and discourages weed germination.

used to surface the soil in rock gardens. These, too, are easily spread and useful for giving crisp surface drainage yet helping to keep the soil below cool and moist, as well as deterring weeds.

Organic Mulches

It is the organic mulches that are usually best, however. At the end of the season they can be worked into the soil to augment its stock of humus. Nor do most of them look out of place - indeed, peat or Forest Bark can actually make a better foil for the plants than the soil itself.

Where suitable, black plastic sheeting can be laid over the soil and seeds sown through holes made in it. Similarly a bed can be covered with a mulch and the material raked to one side wherever seeds are to be sown. Usually, however, organic mulches are put down around growing seedlings when they are a few inches high and are of special benefit to moisture-loving plants. Beware of mulching tender plants too early in the season, because the layer of organic material, if it dries, can act as an insulating blanket. This could prevent the radiation of heat from the soil which helps protect tender plants in the event of a late frost. Remember too, that you should apply the mulch only when the soil is moist, waiting until a rainy period ends or watering the ground first.

Chemical Control of Weeds

There are two types of chemicals that can be used to control weeds when raising plants from seed. The first, sold under the name of Weedol, destroys all green growth that it touches, but is inactivated on contact with the soil. It can be used to destroy weed seedlings on prepared areas before sowing or planting and, with care to keep it off their leaves, among growing plants. Its effect is much the same as that of hoeing, except that it does not disturb the soil and so there is no chance of bringing more weed seeds into the germinating zone. But its main advantage lies in the fact that, unlike when hoeing, once dosed the weed seedlings die - however wet the soil and whatever the weather that follows application after a few hours.

The other type of chemical, sold under the name of Covershield, affects the soil surface to prevent seedling germination and can be used around most flower and vegetable plant seedlings to keep clean soil weed free for some time. It is important to follow the makers' directions to the letter when using weed control chemicals, both to safeguard your plants and to give the product a chance to be really effective.

Prevent Overcrowding

Leaving seedlings crowded together in the rows can be just as bad as allowing weeds to smother them. They quickly become drawn and lanky as they compete with each other for light. This is why you should take care at sowing time not to scatter the seeds too thickly along the rows to begin with or the seedlings will be jostling each other as they appear. Even with correct sowing you will need to thin out the seedlings, removing the surplus to leave the rest standing an inch (2 cm) or so apart to begin with in most cases.

This initial thinning out is best done as soon as the young plants are just large enough to catch hold of between finger and thumb. By

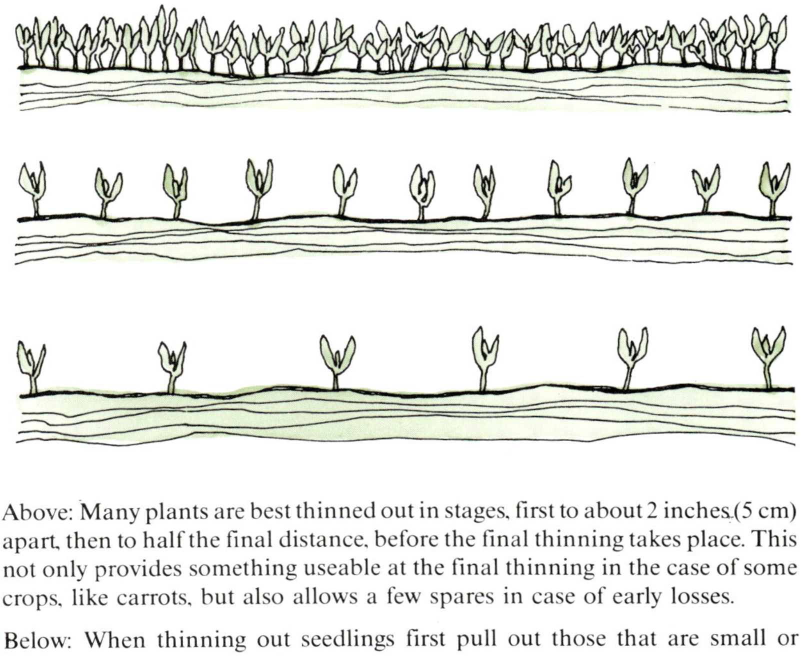

Above: Many plants are best thinned out in stages, first to about 2 inches (5 cm) apart, then to half the final distance, before the final thinning takes place. This not only provides something useable at the final thinning in the case of some crops, like carrots, but also allows a few spares in case of early losses.

Below: When thinning out seedlings first pull out those that are small or malformed, leaving only the strongest to grow on.

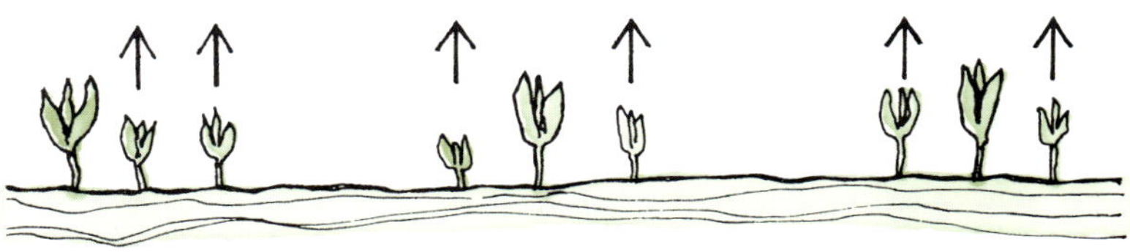

doing it early you not only give your plants a better start but save the root disturbance that is caused to those retained if their immediate neighbours are allowed to develop a large root system before they are pulled up. This first thinning can be a fiddly business, but it does result in better seedlings, even of such things as cabbages grown for planting out later. At the same time as you thin the rows, pull out any weeds growing in them. These, together with the pulled-up plants, are best collected in a bucket as you work and removed from the area.

The first thinning should be followed by a second when the leaves of the plants meet together. At this stage the young plants that were sown where they are to grow and flower or crop can be thinned out to the final distance apart, depending on how much growth they will make. The first sowings of the leafy crops, such as summer spinach and lettuce, however, can be left standing at half the final distance at this second thinning and allowed to develop still further. Then when the final thinning out is done the plants, though nowhere near mature, are large enough to use.

Carrots are rather a different proposition when it comes to thinning them since it depends on what you are aiming for. If you want large roots they are best thinned out to about 2 in (5 cm) apart in

Lettuce and spinach provide useful pickings at the final thinning stage if first left standing at half the final distance until their leaves touch.

the rows when the seedlings are little more than 1 in (2 cm) high. But provided they were sown sparsely to begin with there is no need to thin them out at all. They manage to grow perfectly well much closer together in most garden soils and though the roots are smaller the weight harvested per row can be greater. Many gardeners also wait until the young roots are large enough to use before starting to thin them by pulling the largest ones first. This is fine if you intend to use the whole row as the roots increase in size. It is not a wise practice to follow where you intend to leave some to bulk up for winter storage, because thinning at this stage often encourages an attack of rootfly.

Thin Out or Transplant?

How you treat the seedlings of hardy perennial and biennial plants that will eventually be moved to their flowering positions depends on how many you need. Should you require only a few of any one kind and the rows are long enough you can thin them out to 6-9 in (15-23 cm) apart according to their vigour and leave them where they are to develop until the autumn. Should you require more plants than the rows will hold, some seedlings can be transplanted into another plot and grown on. Whenever possible water them a day beforehand if the weather is dry. Then lift them with the aid of a trowel, keeping plenty of soil around their roots and try to replant them so they are buried no deeper than before once the soil is made firm about them. Always water in the transplanted seedlings, even if the soil does seem moist, because this helps resettle the soil about their roots. Moved with care in this way they will hardly notice the move.

Thinning and transplanting are jobs that ideally should be done in showery weather when the moisture in the air and soil can help offset the inevitable root damage that occurs. Few people can pick and choose the ideal conditions and most of us must do the job when we have the time and opportunity. But it is sensible to move plants in the evening rather than in the heat of the day, also to water in advance the area into which they are to be set out if the soil is dry.

Leeks and onions are out of the ordinary because they make long unbranching roots. What is more, once the roots are broken they become useless and the plants immediately set about making a new set. Because of this it is pointless to give them the same treatment as other plants. Instead they should be lifted with care, after loosening the ground around them, and the soil shaken from their roots which are then cut back. In the case of onions leave the roots about 1 in (2 cm) long so that they can be 'trapped' in the soil to hold the plant upright with the base of it just below the surface. In the case of leeks the roots are best trimmed off about ⅛-¼ in (2.5-5 mm) from the base.

Using a Nursery Bed

Wallflowers and many other common biennial flowers are best moved to a nursery bed where they can be grown on until the display beds are emptied at the end of summer. When the seedlings are large enough to handle comfortably, prepare them for the move by watering them the day beforehand. Lift the seedlings with the aid of a hand fork (top) to avoid root damage. Gently separate them and set them out about 9 inches (23 cm) apart (above).

Using a trowel to make the holes. Hold the plants so that they will be at the same depth as before, then clamp the soil firmly about their roots by levering it against them (above). Afterwards give them a thorough watering to ensure the soil is properly settled about the seedlings and speed their recovery.

of the plant and the leaves shortened to about two thirds of their length. To replant leek seedlings they are simply dropped into 6 in (15 cm) deep holes made with a dibber and watered in by filling the holes to the brim once. Incidentally, both leeks and onions make all their leaves on opposite sides of their stems. Therefore if you take the trouble to arrange the plants with their leaves pointing along the rows, you will be able to move between them more easily later when hoeing and weeding.

When to Water

Provided the soil was properly prepared beforehand and the seedlings thinned out in good time and kept weed free they are unlikely to lack water or food for some time. Even on sandy soil seedlings will thrive for weeks without rain or watering if it was really moist to begin with. Although the surface inch or two (2-5 cm) may dry out due to wind and sun, the moisture reserves deeper down remain there until tapped by plant roots which then suck it dry. An area kept completely bare until June will still have a surprising moisture content 6 in (15 cm) down. As the seedlings grow and demand more moisture, however, there eventually comes a time when they are better for being watered. But this point is reached before they are so short of moisture that they will wilt in bright sunshine.

It is difficult for a home gardener to assess when this stage is reached. Dryness on the surface is no indication of the state of the soil below. The only way to judge therefore, without experience of the particular plot, is occasionally to dig a hole to see how moist the soil is. An alternative, and much easier, is to use an electronic meter of the type sold for testing the moisture needs of pot plants. Having a probe to push into the soil a number of readings can be quickly made to show the dryness or otherwise of different areas about 6 in (15 cm) below the surface.

When water is given it is essential that sufficient is supplied to wet the top 10-12 in (25-30 cm) of soil. Then the plot can be left for a further period of 7-12 days before more is needed. Applying water in such quantities, which can be anything from 3-6 gallons per sq yd (14-27 litres per sq m), according to the soil's capacity for holding moisture, calls for a hosepipe and an efficient sprinkler that can be left unattended in one spot for some time. Where the plants have sufficient foliage almost to cover the ground an oscillating sprinkler is probably best. For smaller plants a type that creates a mist-like spray is better because it does not pound down the soil surface or splash mud over the seedlings. Such a sprinkler covers a much smaller area at a time and consequently needs to be moved more frequently.

Small areas can be watered efficiently with a can, but there is a danger of merely applying only enough water to wet the top inch or two (2-5 cm). This encourages root development chiefly near the surface. Then, when the surface does dry out young plants suffer

Applying water in adequate quantities calls for a hosepipe and an efficient sprinkler that can be left unattended.

more than ever. Proper watering will encourage deep penetrating roots as well, which are necessary for any plant to garner a full ration of moisture and food for itself under normal conditions.

Extra Feeding

Extra feeding of seedlings is usually unnecessary if the soil is reasonably fertile and you added a general fertiliser when preparing the ground. An exception is a vegetable crop such as cauliflowers, which are gross feeders, and may need extra feeding if they are to make a good size. Certainly most flowering plants do not need additional nutrients and, in the case of hardy annuals, too much food could spoil them, encouraging the growth of foliage at the expense of flowers.

There are occasions, however, when the growth of seedlings falters, perhaps due to a pest attack or when the soil temperature is too low in

Foliar feeding, with a soluble fertiliser dissolved in water, is particularly beneficial where there are soil problems.

spring for speedy root development. At such times a supplementary feed to boost their growth can be useful. The quickest response then is gained by foliar feeding. A special soluble fertiliser is dissolved in water and sprayed over the foliage of the plants, which absorb it through their leaves and put it to immediate use. It is especially beneficial where soil problems are the cause of the trouble. In other cases ordinary liquid feeding, where the food is dissolved in water given to the plants, can be done; but the plants are a little slower to react, especially if the food is in a form that must be broken down by soil organisms before the plants can take it up.

Applying dry fertiliser to the soil as a top dressing, by scattering it over the surface between plants, then hoeing or cultivating to mix it in, is rarely called for except on two occasions. The first is on light soils where, in a very wet season, much of the soluble plant food can be leached out by the water draining through the soil and may need to be replaced. The second is in the early spring when the seedlings overwintered in the garden frequently need a fillip to get them going again.

Seedling Pests

The most damaging pest of seedlings are slugs. Indeed, their attacks can be devastating on some plots. Where they abound these nocturnal feeders can clear whole rows of seedlings in a single night so effectively that a weekend gardener may never realise any seedlings came up at all, and blame poor seed for the trouble! Slugs and the related snails are often found in the greatest numbers in gardens bounded by an old wall which provides plenty of hiding places for them. And although these pests seem to be very slow-moving they can travel a surprising distance in an hour. The only way to check how bad a problem they may be on your own plot is to go out at night with a torch and look for them.

During the day slugs hide away and you can often find them gathered under low-growing plants, stones, pieces of wood and plant debris. As a first step in their control, therefore, keep your garden tidy. And where slugs are a serious problem it pays to scatter slug bait over newly sown ground immediately, or as soon as the seedlings appear. A bait containing a substance called methiocarb, rather than the older metaldehyde-based ones, seems to be more effective, though

Slugs and snails can take a heavy toll of seedlings, so it pays to scatter slug bait around young plants and seedbeds as a matter of routine.

more expensive. There is a liquid metaldehyde formulation that can be watered over plants and the surrounding soil to affect the pests as they move in to the attack. Both baits and sprays should be renewed regularly in wet weather.

Slug Traps

As an alternative to chemical control, slugs can be trapped. All you need to do is put down attractive things for them to hide under, such as the rinds of half grapefruits or oranges, or a few succulent cabbage leaves. There are also a few plastic traps available that have to be baited with a little beer or other liquid that is attractive to slugs. The traps must be examined every day and the slugs disposed of. This is a messy business to say the least, but anyone with a severe slug problem soon learns to become hard-hearted.

Another serious seedling pest is the flea beetle. This is a tiny black and yellow striped beetle which can jump quite a long way - hence its name. So small is it that many people do not notice it, but the silvery puncture marks made where it sucks sap from the leaves can be clearly seen. Fortunately this pest is very selective in its feeding and does not attack all plants. Its main source of food are the seedlings of turnips, cabbages and all their relations, including wallflowers and alyssum. It will also attack beetroot and spinach beet quite badly, and has been known to wipe out rhubarb seedlings. Turnips seem to be its most favoured food and if this pest is about you will find it there from the moment the turnips appear. Attacks are always worst when the soil is hot and dry and, when really serious, can kill seedlings completely. Wherever seedling growth appears to be faltering therefore, whatever the plant, check for this pest. The puncture marks on the young leaves are unmistakable. Fortunately, flea beetles are one of the easiest pests to control. All you need to do is puff derris dust along the rows of seedlings, or spray them with any product recommended for this purpose. With the exception of turnips and cauliflowers that can still be attacked when much older, once the young seedlings make their first true leaves, flea beetles no longer seem to worry them.

The other major garden pests very rarely cause problems with young seedlings, the only possible exception being greenfly, which

When dusting plants the aim should be to cover them with a barely discernible layer, not coat them thickly. It is a job best done early or late in the day when the air is often comparatively still.

may appear on quite young seedlings of such plants as China asters sown outdoors in late May. The first sign of trouble is usually a puckering or curling of the leaves, when an inspection will reveal the culprits on the undersides. When discovered clear these pests promptly by spraying the plants with a suitable insecticide. If not treated in time plant growth will falter and development may be permanently impaired.

Protection from Birds

Birds can be a major pest of seedlings, but the habit of attacking them varies from area to area. In some places young peas are regularly pecked about by sparrows; in others it is the lettuce that are the sufferers. Pigeons frequently do enormous damage to brassica seedlings as well early in the year. Apart from this type of direct attack, birds can be a nuisance almost by accident in dry weather if they decide to have a dust bath in the middle of a hitherto neat seedbed.

Prevent birds tearing at seedlings by covering the rows with pea guards, or stringing black cotton over them.

There are bird-repellent sprays that can be applied to plants to deter birds from pecking them but these usually need frequent renewal in wet weather. Wire mesh pea guards provide substantial protection from bird damage, and so does black cotton strung between sticks and criss-crossed over the area. Wire or plastic mesh laid flat on the soil stops birds taking a dust bath. The mesh must be lifted soon after the seedlings appear.

Cats, too, can ruin a seedbed and uproot or bury quite large seedlings with their delvings if they decide to 'spend a penny' there. Again, some form of mesh covering will keep them off, and keeping the area moist by regularly watering it can deter cats in dry weather. Fresh pepper dust and repellent sprays can also be of help. But in a small town garden, where the cat trouble so often seems to be worst, it is a real battle and netting seems to be the best answer.

Rural Pests

In rural areas rabbits can be a menace, especially to anyone living close to a railway line where rabbits are allowed to breed unchecked. Even a single rabbit can do great damage in a night or two grazing along the seedlings. The only lasting answer to this problem is to surround the whole plot with a 2 ft (60 cm) high fence, constructed

Use wire mesh guards over newly sown areas where necessary to keep off cats and birds, both of which can seriously disturb the soil.

from 3 ft (90 cm) wide small mesh wire netting, the bottom 6 in (15 cm) of which is bent outwards at right angles and buried 6 in (15 cm) deep to prevent rabbits burrowing under it. It is an expensive business, as I know to my cost, but it needs to be properly done only once to give you absolute protection for many years.

Mice and shrews can be other annoying pests, but chiefly where peas are concerned. Where a plot borders open fields or rough ground they can clear whole rows of early sowings quite quickly to the point where you may have no more than four of five plants come up in a 25 ft (7.5 m) row. The tell-tale signs are the neat, tapering funnel-shaped holes where they dig down to extract the seeds. To deter these predators and birds from taking them, you can soak the seeds in paraffin overnight before sowing them; this treatment does not seem to affect their powers of germination. The only alternative is to set traps for the mice - but do put them either in a drainpipe or under a tunnel made from bricks so that small birds cannot be caught in them.

4. Raising Seedlings Under Glass

The use of a greenhouse or cold frame, with their controlled environment, considerably widens the field of plants that you can raise from seed - while the provision of extra warmth enormously extends the scope of what you can grow. It not only gives the opportunity to attempt many half-hardy plants that - though they will happily grow out of doors in summer months - cannot stand frost and must be sown in warmth, but also those exotic types that must be protected throughout their lives. Apart from these, glass protection is needed to raise with success many hardy plants whose seed is too tiny or too slow-developing to be raised with any degree of certainty in open ground. It is also sensible to sow under glass the more expensive seeds, like those of F1 hybrids, in order to get the best possible results.

Although often regarded as the poor man's greenhouse, a cold frame offers special advantages over a greenhouse when raising hardy plants from seed that are slow to germinate. A frame is most essential, too, for acclimatising those plants raised in warmth that are to be finally set out in the garden. When it is equipped with some sort of heating system there is little that cannot be raised in a frame. In theory, therefore, a frame is more versatile than a greenhouse, but by no means as convenient. In practice the ability actually to work and look after tender seedlings within a greenhouse, regardless of the weather outside, means that they are more efficiently looked after.

What You Can Grow

What you can reasonably expect to raise from seed under glass depends, of course, on the degree of warmth that can be maintained. And there is no doubt that the ability to raise plants in pots and seed trays, even in an unheated greenhouse, greatly increases your scope. You should have little difficulty with those hardy plants that are rarely successful when sown out of doors (see Appendix 2), because they need no heat, only patience and attention to detail. Their ranks include those with very small seeds, or seedlings that are very slow to develop after germination, and a surprisingly wide variety that for one reason or another have delayed germination. These will be perfectly happy in a well-ventilated cold frame, where the top is merely used to protect them from heavy downpours of rain, or even under open-ended cloches. All you really do, in fact, is to prevent them being lost, hoed or dug up by accident, or swamped by weeds before they can appear and develop into reasonable-sized plants that can be planted out and grown on like any other. Given the use of a cold greenhouse, you can get quicker results with some hardy plants.

On the vegetable front lettuce, cauliflowers, cabbages and onions are examples of crops that can be raised from seed sown a month or so earlier in the year than would be possible out of doors, the seedlings being grown on in pots and boxes and later planted out to provide extra early crops. Even earlier as well as more certain results are possible if a little artificial warmth can be provided just to germinate the seeds. An airing cupboard is useful for this purpose, but as soon as the seedlings appear they *must* be moved into the light.

An unheated greenhouse or frame is ideal, too, for raising half-hardy vegetables and flowers. These are the plants that can be grown in open ground once the danger of frost is passed. They include such crops as courgettes, marrows and sweet corn sown from mid- to late April. Also the quicker-developing bedding plants, of which French and African marigolds, nemesia and zinnias are examples. Sown at the beginning of April, germinated in warmth and grown on in an unheated greenhouse until planting out time in late May they can make a splendid show. Slower to develop bedding plants, like lobelia and matricaria, can be raised in this way also but then begin flowering later than usual. For a full summer display these are better raised in warmer conditions.

Advantages of Heating

It is the ability to maintain a minimum temperature of 50F (10C) early in the year that really provides you with the best possibilities for raising many exotic plants. Sowing can then be started in a heated propagator where an even higher temperature can be held for seed germination and development to the stage where the first move is called for. From then on most seedlings can be grown in cooler conditions in a greenhouse (for preference) or frame. This offers scope to raise all except, perhaps, the trickiest of bedding plants like scarlet salvias, while in May when the average greenhouse temperature will be much higher, you can make a start with tender greenhouse and house plants, such as gloxinias and African violets.

Lacking heat, there is no point in sowing these temperature-conscious plants before May or June, and even then you have the problem of keeping the seedlings that are not winter dormant during cold months. Many hardy border plants commonly raised from seed, like lupins and delphiniums, quickly make sizeable plants and flower during the first summer if raised in early warmth.

No matter whether the plants are hardy or exotic, growing them in a warm greenhouse or raising in a cold frame the technique of preparing the containers and sowing the seeds is common to almost all of them.

Raising plants under glass demands a very different attitude to raising them out in the open. Although the scope is greater due to the fact that the environment can be controlled to provide greater warmth or humidity, *you* have to do the controlling. A greenhouse cannot be neglected for days at a time - at least not unless ventilation, heating and watering are automatic. And though plant development is much quicker in extra warmth, the congenial conditions also

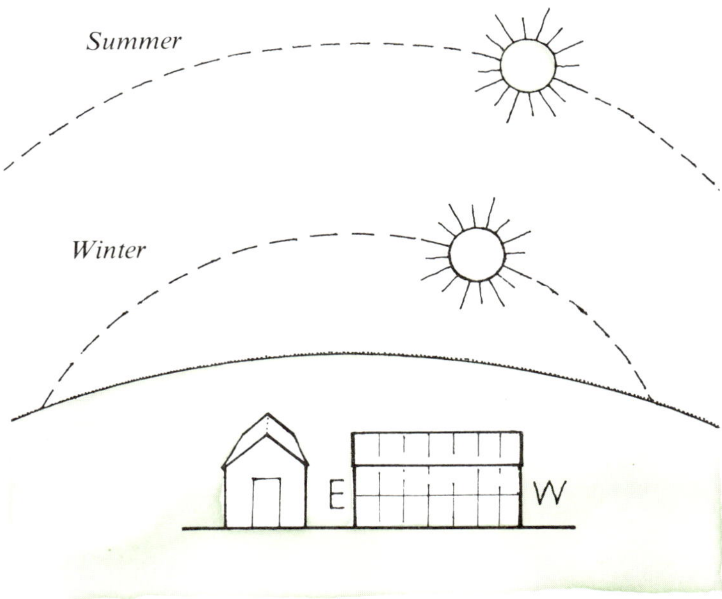

Efficiency of light penetration depends on the angle of the sun to the glass of a greenhouse. In late winter and spring when the sun is low in the sky there is an advantage in having a greenhouse sited east to west, especially when it is used mainly for propagation. In summer, however, when the sun is high a north/south orientation is better. Where a greenhouse has to serve a number of purposes and contains plants of different heights, siting it north to south is generally the best compromise.

encourage pests and diseases as well. For these reasons a greenhouse should be visited at least twice a day - which is why a site at the far end of the garden is not the best place for it! - and the needs of the seedlings dealt with promptly.

For general use a greenhouse and frame should be placed where they receive good light early in the year. Lack of light can be a factor that limits plant growth at that time, even in a heated structure. Light provides the energy which all green-leaved plants use to manufacture food in their leaves. Lack of light, especially when coupled with too high a temperature, results in pale, weak, spindly seedlings. It can be an advantage, however, to have a second frame sited where it is shielded from direct sun in the summer, but not overshadowed to the point where the light is very dim. This shaded frame can be most useful for growing on seedlings of such plants as hardy primulas and greenhouse cinerarias which much prefer cool conditions in summer.

Greenhouse Management

Although a greenhouse offers great possibilities for growing tender plants from seed, the mere ownership of one does not confer automatic success. You must be able to manage it efficiently to create and maintain a suitable environment inside. The chief controlling factors are warmth, light and atmospheric humidity - and these must be balanced if plants are to flourish. Early in the year when the angle of the sun is low and the days short, the amount of available light can limit the plant development, as I have just explained. An obvious precaution to take, therefore, is to keep the glass as clean as possible by washing it regularly from the time you make the first sowings of the year. It is amazing how much grime can accumulate on it in two or three weeks.

Later, in the summer, the temperature may rise too high for some plants to grow well and, when coupled with high light intensity, may even scorch their leaves. Ventilation to gain a constant change of air is essential then. Just opening the roof ventilators is not enough; you need side ventilators as well to let in cooler air and allow a circulation to occur. At such times it is impossible to keep temperatures to a reasonable level in a small garden greenhouse by ventilation alone, and some form of greenhouse shading must be employed. This is best arranged in the form of external blinds that can be rolled down and up as required. Alternatively, a liquid type of shading material can be sprayed or painted on the glass. White is best since it does not tend to filter out the very light rays that plants need most. That marketed under the name of Coolglass is very good since it is not easily washed away by the rain, yet can readily be removed from the glass when it is dry by rubbing it off with a cloth.

Keep up Humidity

The increased air change due to extra ventilation needed to keep down the greenhouse temperature in hot weather also reduces the atmospheric humidity and the air can become too dry. This can lead to an increase in the watering needs of plants, encourage red spider mites that attack plants, as well as slowing down growth in many cases. Plants are also more likely to suffer from heat scorch in dry air. The supply of moisture to evaporate can be improved by damping down the path and benches two or three times a day. It helps in summer if the benches and concrete floor are surfaced with sand or shingle that can be wetted to provide a more lasting supply of moisture. A greenhouse well stocked with plants also tends to be more humid, since the plants give off moisture through the pores in their leaves to help in this respect.

On the other hand a period of wet weather in summer, which results in high humidity outside the greenhouse, makes control of humidity inside extremely difficult. Where heat can be applied to keep the air buoyant, this will help reduce condensation. In unheated structures little can be done except to take adequate steps to prevent diseases by spraying or fumigation.

During cold weather, and especially in unheated structures, excessive humidity should be guarded against since, as temperatures fall, moisture in the air can condense on to the plants and encourage attacks of grey mould (botrytis) and other diseases. In the colder months, therefore, any necessary watering is best done in the morning, taking care not to splash water about. Every suitable opportunity should also be taken to ventilate a greenhouse at this time to get rid of over-moist air. Condensation is less of a problem in heated greenhouses because the warmer the air the more moisture it can hold. Even so, efforts should be made to keep down humidity. To recap briefly, in early spring ventilation should be assessed according to the needs of maintaining warmth, yet removing unwanted humidity. As the season progresses, more ventilation is needed to keep down temperatures. When a great deal of ventilation is needed, the humidity needs to be boosted to prevent the air from becoming too dry.

Where a heating system is installed it should be used to maintain a suitable minimum temperature in spring and its use will be less as the season advances. A little artificial heating can be valuable in wet summer periods, however, to prevent moisture condensing out on plants. Generally speaking plants enjoy much the same conditions as we do. If you feel uncomfortable in a greenhouse your plants are likely to be uncomfortable as well.

Looking after a frame is just the same as looking after a greenhouse, except that you cannot experience the conditions inside. But a frame does have the advantage that, because its top can be removed completely, it can be more efficiently ventilated to keep down the temperature within. Indeed, for much of the year the top can be left off completely and replaced merely to provide weather protection.

Need for Hygiene

Owing to the warmer, moister conditions under glass, pests and especially diseases are greatly encouraged and scrupulous attention should be paid to simple hygiene in the greenhouse. As it is true of so many gardening problems, prevention is always much better than cure. Where possible the structure and benches should be thoroughly washed down and cleaned once a year, preferably in winter just before the first sowings of the new season are made. At no time should rubbish be allowed to accumulate; plant debris provides inevitable breeding grounds for disease, while piles of dirty pots, seed trays and other items provide hiding places for pests such as woodlice and earwigs. By simply keeping a greenhouse clean and tidy you can save yourself a great deal of trouble.

It is essential, too, to use clean containers and materials when seed sowing. Dirty pots and seed trays can carry diseases in the old compost adhering to them, so do wash them clean before you even begin to open a seed packet. Modern plastic containers have a great advantage in being non-porous, smooth and easy to wash.

Even more important is to use a disease- and pest-free compost in which to sow seeds and grow your seedlings. *Never use soil straight from the garden*: to do so is to court disaster. Apart from the fact that garden soil is liable to introduce pests and diseases, it rarely has a texture that allows it to drain properly once wetted in a container, and frequently sets brick-hard as it dries out. Although it can be sterilised and mixed with other ingredients, such as sand and peat, to form a more suitable potting and sowing 'compost', as such mixtures are called, most home gardeners find it more convenient, certain, and thus more economical in the end, to buy a proprietary seed or potting compost when raising plants.

Types of Compost

Proprietary composts can broadly be divided into two groups. The first, which are known as John Innes (J I) composts, are soil based. They are, or should be, prepared according to the strict formulae devised at the John Innes Horticultural Research Institute many years ago, which were the first 'standard' composts devised. They are prepared from a mixture of sterilised loam, peat and sand with added fertilisers. Their success depends on the quality of the loam used and in the past have proved very variable, with the result that these composts fell into disrepute. In an effort to get back to the proper standards, the J I Manufacturers' Association was formed and unless you have a trustworthy local supplier it is wise to look for the Association's Seal of Approval on any bag of John Innes compost when buying it. The second group of composts comprises those which are peat based, and there is a large number of different brands on the market. They have the advantage of being light in weight and pleasant to handle.

The type of compost to use is largely a matter of personal choice. Some people prefer one to the other, but all are capable of giving excellent results when used correctly. For the general run of plant raising I favour peat composts because I believe they result in better root development. However, for long-term germination in particular, such as where I expect to have to wait for the dormancy of seeds to be broken by frost before they will grow, I prefer to use a soil-based compost. This is because the loam will hold on to some food value in the compost long after the peat has lost the lot.

The main thing to beware of when using peat composts is not to over-compress them. If you do each container can turn into a miniature bog that is too soggy to encourage good root development. In the case of soil composts it is essential to ensure that the containers drain freely from the base or they, too, can remain soggy and become sour. When lightly firmed, peat compost is very free-draining and well aerated, so much so that it is difficult to overwater it. It is this extra aeration, I believe, that encourages such good root development in seedlings.

Other points to remember about peat composts are that when they run out of food they do so quickly - there is nothing gradual about it - and regular feeding must then be started promptly. Also, it is the water absorbed by the compost that gives pots stability - unlike the heavier soil composts - so that when the peat dries out it becomes very light, and tall plants in small pots easily topple over.

Composts are further classified as 'sowing' or 'potting' composts. Because the seedlings live off the food stored in the seed at first, they do not require a rich medium in which to germinate. Indeed, in some instances the presence of fertiliser can actually inhibit germination. So where germination is swift and the seedlings will be pricked out shortly after they appear, a sowing compost, which contains a little food, suits them well. The majority of quick-growing plants germinate as well in potting compost as they do in a special seed one. This not only saves having to use two different composts, but also ensures that the seedlings have a ready supply of food should their first move to other containers be delayed for any reason. At least one brand of peat compost is sold for both seed sowing and potting.

John Innes compost is sold in three grades: No 1, No 2, and No 3, as well as the seed compost (J I S). The fertiliser content of the No 1 grade is doubled and tripled respectively to produce the other two. J I No 1 can be used when sowing a wide variety of plants, especially the more vigorous seedlings, such as tomatoes and cucumbers, that would be potted on using J I No 2. Sowing in J I S is to be preferred, however, for sowings made in January or February, when the natural light is poor.

Although normal composts are suitable for a very wide range of plants, an exception has to be made for those which hate lime. For these a special lime-free medium should be used, such as that sold for azaleas and ericaceous plants, and which can usually be had from the larger stores and garden centres. If you live in an area where there is lime in the mains water supply - which is said to be 'hard' - you should water such plants and their seeds with rain water instead.

Keep to the Same Type

Whichever of the two main types of compost you decide to use to raise a batch of plants, do keep to the same type. If you re-pot a seedling that has been grown in a peat compost by using a soil-based medium, or vice versa, you will have all sorts of watering problems because of the different draining and drying rates of the two materials. When it comes to setting young plants out of doors, however, I find those raised in peat transplant very well if given a thorough soaking beforehand. Indeed, they frequently continue growing with no visible check.

Choice of Containers

The chief containers used for seed raising are pots and seed trays, the size depending on how many seedlings you intend to raise. For germinating just a few seeds a 3 in or 3½ in (8 or 9 cm) diameter pot is adequate. But the shallower 5 in (12.5 cm) dwarf pot, which requires less compost than a full-sized one, is useful for a greater number of seeds. Thereafter it is better to use small or large seed trays. The only seed trays worth having, in my opinion, are strong plastic ones. They are easy to clean, nest neatly together for storage and, with careful handling, last for many seasons.

Most of the pots I use are plastic ones, again for easy cleaning and storing and the fact that they are light in weight. You find an advantage in their lightness, especially if they are filled with peat compost, when carrying trays of them from greenhouse to frame, or out into the garden when it is time to set out young plants growing in them. Being non-porous, plastic pots dry out less quickly than clay pots, which can of course still be bought in many garden centres. What is more, it can be easier to remove plants from plastic pots if they have been growing in them for some time, because the roots cannot hold on to the sides as they can to clay pots.

Use for Clay Pots

Anyone who raises a wide variety of plants from seed will find that clay pots do have one special use. This is for seeds of hardy plants which you expect to take a long time to germinate. If the pots are filled with J I compost they can be buried in a frame up to their rims in a bed of moist peat, sand or ashes. Provided you keep this 'plunge bed' - as it is called - damp, water will be absorbed through the sides of the pots to keep the soil inside evenly moist and cool. This avoids any possibility of disturbing the seeds or tiny seedlings that might occur if the pots had to be individually watered. It also saves time by reducing the frequency of watering.

Where the seeds are large enough to handle they can be sown individually in Fyba or peat pots which can be had in various sizes. These offer the advantage in that the seedling can be planted or potted without any root disturbance since they can be set out pot-and-all. The fibrous pot quickly breaks down when surrounded with moist soil and compost to allow roots to grow through it. In fact, you can often see white root tips poking through before they are planted. It is essential, however, to water such pots thoroughly before planting and also water the plants in well afterwards. These pots come in a variety of sizes. Fyba also produce 'growing tubes' which are long, slim pots, ideal for such plants as sweet peas that quickly make long roots. Not the least of their attraction is that they do away with pot washing and storage.

Soil Blocks

You can, of course, dispense with pots altogether, by using compressed blocks of compost instead. Fisons sell a special tool and blocking compost for making your own. Until such blocks are well filled with roots they must be handled as little as possible and are best spaced out in polythene-lined trays as they are made so that they can be moved together in batches without your having to touch them. A different variation on this theme is offered by Jiffy 7s. These are compressed discs of compost that swell up when watered to make a full-sized block surrounded with plastic mesh. Like Fyba and peat pots, compost blocks enable you to set out seedlings with a minimum of root disturbance, which is specially useful when dealing with such plants as sweet corn or zinnias, that object to having their roots disturbed in any way.

Similar, too, are the various compartmented trays and tray dividers that are sold. These are filled with compost and seeds or plants set in them. When ready to be moved each seedling can be lifted out in its own separate block of compost with its roots intact.

Apart from the containers that are sold specially for the purpose, people who produce plants to sell on stalls at local fetes and other functions use all manner of disposable cups, tubs and cartons to cut down on cost. Old plastic sandwich boxes, especially if they still have a snap-on lid, are useful seed raisers if a few holes are made in the base with a drill or heated nail. I have seen egg trays, the holes filled with compost, used for raising plants also, and no doubt ingenuity will suggest even more ideas. But do remember that containers should taper wider at the top or at least be straight-sided, or you will have trouble removing the plants when they have grown. And do make sure they are clean, fume-free and uncontaminated with oil or any other substance that could upset seedlings.

Preparing for Sowing

Having obtained a supply of containers and compost to use, the next job is to prepare them for sowing. Whatever the compost it should be nicely moist to the point where if you squeeze a handful of it together it will hold its shape. If it is so dry that it falls apart you will not be able to compress it properly: if too wet it will easily overcompress. Compost should never be so wet that you can wring moisture from it.

When using J I composts you must ensure that the containers can drain freely from the base so that surplus water can quickly escape, unless the containers are to stand on a special self-watering bench. Otherwise there is a danger that the soil at the bottom will stay soggy, become sour and then roots will not grow in it. The traditional method for dealing with clay pots is known as 'crocking'. The crocks, or pieces of broken pot, are arranged in a layer, hollow-side down in the base of the pot, after placing one large crock over the central drainage hole. These crocks are then covered with a little coarse peat, or roughage left in a sieve after sifting the compost before use, to prevent the soil washing down and blocking the drainage channels.

Like the pots, crocks must be clean and washing them used to be the most unpleasant job in the nursery, since it was usually done at a cold time of year. It is not so bad if you can do it in the kitchen sink with warm water. Baking or boiling the crocks is even more effective because then they are sterilised.

When using a soil-based sowing compost, cover the bases of seed trays with broken crocks arranged hollow side down before filling, to ensure surplus water can drain away quickly.

After ensuring the sides and corners are properly filled, roughly level the soil, then create a firm level surface with the aid of a wooden presser.

With plastic pots that have a number of small holes in the base, I use a little clean ½ in (1 cm) gravel as a bottom layer and cover this with roughage. Gravel can also be used in clay pots provided the drainage holes are not too large, in which case you have to use one crock to cover each of them first. In the case of a seed tray, crocks or gravel must be used to cover the slits or holes in the base. Ideally the trays should be 3 in (8 cm) deep, which allows for a ½ in (1 cm) layer of drainage material and 2 in (5 cm) of compost above it, but not many modern trays are made this deep and you may have to settle for slightly less.

Although I used to put in a gravel layer for drainage when I first used peat composts I subsequently found this was unnecessary and no longer make any special provision for drainage at all.

Filling the Containers

Having arranged the drainage layer, fill the container with loose, sifted compost and strike off the surplus level with the rim. Then give the base of the pot or seed tray a sharp rap or two on the bench to settle the soil. The compost in pots can now be pressed down to make a smooth, level surface ¼-½ in (5-10 mm) below the rim. This is easily done with a suitably shaped piece of flat wood fitted with a handle, or you can use the base of another clean pot or tray.

Before pressing down the soil in a tray, however, gently push it down with your fingers around the sides, and especially in the corners where there are often hollows. Then roughly level the compost with your hand before finally pressing it flat and firm. Such attention makes the sides slightly more compact than the centre. If this simple procedure is omitted there is always a danger that the water, when given, will drain quickly out at the sides of the tray leaving the centre dry.

It is important not to over-compress peat compost. Having filled the container very loosely to the brim, only the lightest pressure is needed to create a level surface on which the seeds can be sown, though you do still need to tuck the compost in gently around the sides and corners of a seed tray before the final levelling and firming, as described above.

When to Water

Gardeners have different ideas on when to water. Some prefer to water pots and boxes before sowing, others do the job afterwards. With soil-based composts, provided it is properly moist to begin with there should be enough moisture to trigger the germination of quick-growing seeds, provided you cover the containers to ensure the soil does not dry out after sowing. With peat composts, however, I prefer to water the containers and allow them time to drain before sowing, applying it with a watering can fitted with a very fine rose.

An alternative method, and one which is safer to use after sowing to

Watering by immersion saves disturbing the compost or seeds and is the best way of rewetting overdry compost at any time. Stand the containers in a deep tray of water and leave them to soak until the compost surface darkens with moisture.

avoid washing the seeds together, is to stand the containers in a tray of water which reaches almost as high as the compost surface. Leave them to stand in it until the moisture shows on the surface of the compost when the containers should be removed and allowed to drain. The chief argument against the submersion method is that it tends to wash away plant foods from the soil. But if the compost is rather dry it is a most effective method of re-wetting it and I keep an old, deep baking tray specially for the purpose.

Sowing Techniques under Glass

Once the containers are prepared the next job is to sow the seeds and cover them (except those that will germinate only in light) to the correct depth. The two dangers to avoid are sowing them too thickly and burying them too deeply. Home gardeners generally err by sowing far too many seeds in a pot or box. The result is that the seedlings compete one with another immediately and then quickly become drawn and leggy and are difficult to disentangle. And, once the required number of seedlings has been taken, a great many surplus ones are then thrown away. It is better to sow fewer in the first place, to sow them in a larger tray, or use more than one container to give them more space. The worst fault of all is to sow all the seeds in a packet, whether they are needed or not, in the belief that you will get your money's worth. You will not if it results in spoilt seedlings!

Expert plant propagators who regularly sow a great many boxes of seeds of all types develop almost an instinct for judging the quantity of seed held between finger and thumb and an ability to scatter them evenly over the compost. For less experienced gardeners I am a firm advocate for spacing the seeds individually wherever possible. It may sound a fiddle and does take more time, but it pays dividends in sturdier seedlings while the time is regained later, when they have to be moved individually into other containers to be grown on. Apart from this, it enables you to keep a rough check on the number of seeds sown and ensure you raise neither a great many more nor fewer than you actually need.

I have explained that there are natural reasons why not all seeds are able to grow, and that not all seeds that do grow necessarily produce a healthy seedling. I aim to sow two to three times more seeds than the number of plants I will eventually require. This seems to work well enough with flower and vegetable seeds that have been bred for the purpose. When dealing with unusual and wild plants, however, it is anybody's guess what the germination percentage may be, so here it pays to sow more.

Spacing Them Out

Seeds which are large enough to be handled with ease between finger and thumb are the easiest to deal with. Indeed many, like marrows and sweet peas, are best sown in individual containers. Sow two to three seeds spaced about ½ in (1 cm) apart per pot. If more than one develops the weakest ones can be quickly removed to leave the strongest. This saves having to sow extra pots to allow for any 'misses' where the pot remains annoyingly vacant. Push the seeds about ½ in (1 cm) deep into the compost, which is then pressed over them. It is said to be a good idea to set flat seeds - like those of pumpkins and lilies - on edge, since they are then less likely to rot. While this may be a factor out of doors, if the soil is cold and germination is delayed, it should not make the slightest difference under glass. But it certainly is easier to slip them in sideways than to try and push them in face-side down.

If you come across any really large seeds, like the conkers of a horse chestnut tree for example, they are best sown when preparing the containers by half filling a small pot, then putting in a seed and covering it with the rest of the soil, which can be firmed around it.

The number of seeds that can be handled easily this way is limited but there are a great many more that can be handled with the aid of a

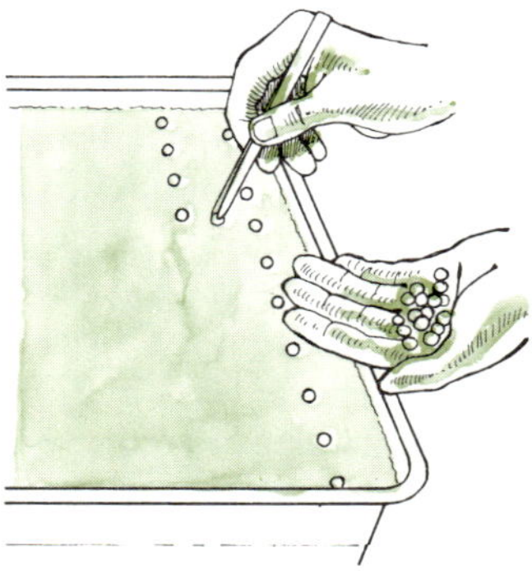

Seeds large enough to pick up individually with tweezers are best spaced out individually to save over-crowding when they emerge.

Small seeds can be scattered over the levelled compost and covered with sifted compost.

pair of tweezers. Space these out ¼-½ in (5-10 mm) apart over the compost. Cover them with a thin layer of compost which has been passed through a fine sieve to remove any lumps or coarse fibres. The depth of this layer is varied according to the seeds, but is generally equivalent in thickness to the seeds themselves. Finally, firm this layer over the seeds so that they are securely anchored in the compost.

Sowing Small Seeds

When the seeds are too small to be handled comfortably, even with tweezers, there is no alternative but to scatter them by hand, holding a pinch between finger and thumb and releasing them gradually while moving your hand above the compost. If the seeds are light coloured you can see fairly easily where they fall. If they are dark coated it can be helpful to sprinkle a little clean, fine sand over the soil first to provide a colour contrast. Seeds of this size generally need no more than the merest scattering of compost over them.

Cover seeds with sifted compost to ensure there are no lumps that might deter, even prevent, emergence of seedlings.

Finally, we come to those seeds that are so tiny that they are packed in a small transparent envelope within the seed packet and frequently resemble a tiny pinch of dust in one corner of it. But do not be misled: there can still be a surprising quantity of seeds there. By far the most effective way I have found of dealing with these minute seeds is to mix them with a little clean (baked) fine builders' sand in a small glass, such as a medicine measure. Use about a rounded teaspoonful (10 ml) of sand for a 5 in (12.5 cm) pot and stir the seeds into it. Scatter the mixture evenly over the surface then press it into contact with the compost. No further covering is needed for such tiny seeds, which are easily smothered. Lobelias, begonias and gloxinias are examples of plants best sown in this way.

Write the labels before sowing the seed, then there is less chance of confusion.

As soon as each container is sown give it a label bearing the name of the plant, sowing date and any other information, such as flower colour and growing height perhaps, that you may require to know later. If you do not do this it is all too easy to get into a muddle, especially when more than one type of the same plant is being grown, such as a trailing and non-trailing lobelia, or petunias of separate colours. Much the easiest way, I find, is to write out the labels before beginning a session of sowing. Then there is no temptation to put off the job.

Once the seeds are sown the containers must on no account be allowed to dry out before the seedlings appear. The best way to keep them moist is to slip each container inside a clean, clear polythene bag, which is then kept closed. Alternatively the top of trays or pots can be covered with clean polythene film closed firmly around the sides with a rubber band; or use clinging film if you prefer. Keep the covering taut so that it cannot droop and touch the compost. Covered

Keep the containers moist by putting them inside a polythene bag.

in this way plastic containers will stay moist for many weeks if necessary, but the coverings must be removed as soon as the seedlings appear. This means examining them at least once a day.

Such covering can be dispensed with if the containers are to be put into a closed propagator, or propagating case, where a high humidity can be maintained. Nor is it required for those pots of seeds sown late in the year and placed out of doors to be exposed to winter weather to break their dormancy (see page 13).

The Next Step

The next step is to find a place to put containers of seed while waiting for them to germinate which depends on the temperature they need (see Appendix 1). For early spring sowings of vegetables and bedding plants a warm greenhouse or frame, though not essential for just a few pots is certainly convenient and really necessary if you are raising plants on any scale. The same is true for those hardy border plants, such as delphiniums and lupins, that will flower in their first season if sown early in warmth. The majority of hardy plants, be they annuals or perennials, germinate naturally and well in an unheated greenhouse or frame.

To avoid the expense of running a complete greenhouse at a sufficiently high temperature to ensure speedy germination, most greenhouse owners use an electric propagator - a sort of self-contained, electrically heated frame. This can be controlled to create an even temperature of 70F (21C) or even higher, while the greenhouse is run at a minimum of 50F (10C). On a small scale it is even possible to germinate many seeds in an airing cupboard. Once up they can be moved out into the cooler greenhouse to grow on.

A capacious heated propagator that holds a quantity of pots and trays is extremely useful when raising tender plants. It enables a high temperature to be maintained for them economically without keeping the whole greenhouse hot.

Such a regime will not suit all tender plants of course, but it can be successful with a surprising number provided you do not sow them too early. A greenhouse run at a minimum temperature of 50F (10C) has a considerably higher *average* temperature. The number of hours when the seedlings actually have to put up with temperatures below 60F (16C) during each 24 hour period can be very few in April if the weather is reasonable. The real restriction, therefore, is not germinating temperature so much as the conditions that you can offer the young seedlings. For this reason there is no point in sowing tender greenhouse or house plants before May, or even June, if you have no large warm area for the seedlings. By that time an ordinary unheated greenhouse should be warm enough for all except the really temperature-conscious plants.

5. Aftercare of Seedlings

Once the seedlings appear any plastic covering must be removed to ensure they enjoy fresh air and, early in the year, the maximum light available. From then on they will also require watering. This must be done with great care if the seedlings are not to be flattened, spattered with mud, or buried by soil disturbance. In the majority of cases using a watering can, preferably of the Haws pattern and fitted with a fine rose, is effective. Turn the rose so that holes face upwards; this gives a very fine, gentle spray. For the tiniest seedlings, as well as pots and boxes that show signs of drying out before germination occurs, it is much safer to apply water as a 'mist spray' by means of a small pump-up hand sprayer. This may take a little longer, but ensures the seedlings are never swamped nor the compost disturbed.

Pricking Out

Once the seedlings are large enough to handle, those sown together in pots or boxes need to be given more space and compost in which to develop. This is done by transplanting them - 'pricking out' is the gardener's term for it - into other pots, or more often, seed trays. These are filled with potting compost and prepared the same way as for

Always handle seedlings by their leaves when pricking out, never by the stem which is easily bruised.

Where large seeds have been well spaced out they can usually be moved with plenty of compost around their roots.

sowing. In this case, however, it is imperative to ensure there is about ½ in (1 cm) of space between the container rim and the compost surface to hold water later on.

Small pots and seedlings can be completely turned out and the tiny plants gently separated to avoid root damage as far as possible. Those in large pots or trays can be dug out in groups and a blunt knife is handy for the purpose. Provided the seedlings are not over-crowded it is not difficult to part them by a combination of gently crumbling the compost and pulling them apart. Only handle seedlings by holding their leaves, never their stems which are very fragile. If a leaf is bruised the seedling usually survives, but if the stem is damaged it will die. Seedlings seem to make a great deal more root growth in peat than soil composts, and this makes it more difficult to separate them without damage, especially if you wait too long; but seedlings can lose a surprising amount of root yet still grow away without difficulty.

As you separate the seedlings, set each in the new container, making a hole for it with a small dibber - a suitably sized, bluntly pointed piece of wood. Hold the seedling by a leaf so that its root dangles in the hole, then press the soil firm about it. After planting the 'seed leaves' - the first pair of leaves to appear after germination - should just sit on the soil. If a seedling has a very long root that cannot be contained in the hole without being bent, tweak off the end of it between finger and thumb. As each container is filled give it a thorough watering to help settle the compost.

Patching Out

Some very tiny seedlings such as those of begonias or lobelia, take ages to reach a size that can be handled. To save them being drawn up due to overcrowding they are usually 'patched out'. That is, they are

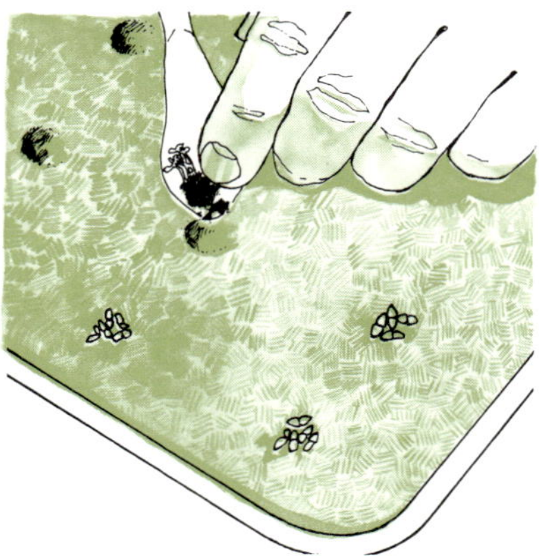

Tiny, slow-growing seedlings, such as those of begonia and lobelia, are best 'patched-out' at first in small groups. From then on each group can be treated as one plant, or split up later when the seedlings are large enough to handle individually.

moved in small groups and spaced out in another box. Later, when the seedlings are larger, the groups can be separated. But where growing, say, lobelia of one colour, the groups can be treated and grown as though they were single plants.

Whether or not you prick out seedlings into boxes, or individually into small pots depends on how fast they will grow and your ultimate aim. It can be more economical of space and compost to raise in boxes anything that is to be planted out of doors unless they grow very large quite quickly. Plants that are to be grown in pots in a greenhouse or indoors are generally best pricked out into small pots to begin with. An exception are the very slow developers, which would not make use of all the compost in their pots within a few weeks. These are best grown fairly close together in boxes for a while, then moved into small pots. There is no doubt that, if the best quality plant is your aim, the majority of seedlings do best when given individual pots, which not only gives them more compost but avoids serious root disturbance when they are eventually re-potted or planted out.

In the average box of home-grown plants the seedlings vary a great deal in size. In part this is due to the fact that many people are loth to grade their plants for size when pricking them out. The larger the seedling is, the more food it can produce and the quicker it grows. All other factors being equal, a large seedling will continue to outstrip its fellows in development.

Therefore it is sensible when pricking out two or more trays of one type of plant to grade the seedlings, keeping the largest together in one box, the smaller in another. Beware of doing this if you are raising a mixed batch, however. Not all species develop at the same rate and, in some cases, even seedlings of the same type of plant with different flower colour may have slightly differing germination times and

Equal spacing when they are pricked out is essential if the seedlings are to develop evenly. A Dibalot helps to this end by compressing and marking the compost in one go. Unwanted holes are easily erased.

development rates. If you grade these you may not finish up with a proper colour mixture. Even worse, should you reject the smallest ones you may lack one colour altogether.

The other chief causes of uneven development of a tray of plants are uneven consolidation of the compost which results in one part of the box drying out more rapidly, or standing the trays on an uneven surface so that the water tends to drain down one side or end. Under normal conditions the food available in compost lasts about six weeks, depending on the frequency of watering and speed at which the plants develop and extract it. After that they must be moved into a larger container and given some fresh compost, planted out, or fed with some sort of general plant food, which is most easily done by mixing it with the water you give them. In the case of plants that are to be grown on in pots, the really vigorous growing ones, such as tomatoes, can be moved into the final, largest size at this stage. However, the majority of plants are best moved into pots 1-2 in (2-5 cm) larger each time until they are in the size that suits them in maturity. If given too much fresh compost at a time there is always the danger that the soil may lose its goodness before the roots have time to explore it. Indeed it can become so poor that roots refuse even to grow into it.

Potting Off and Potting On

Moving seedlings into pots for the first time is known as 'potting off'. Pots of 3-3½ in (8-9 cm) size are prepared by first arranging any necessary drainage layer in the base (see page 77). For small seedlings - those of tomatoes for instance - the pots are filled with potting compost and firmed in much the same way as for seed sowing. A

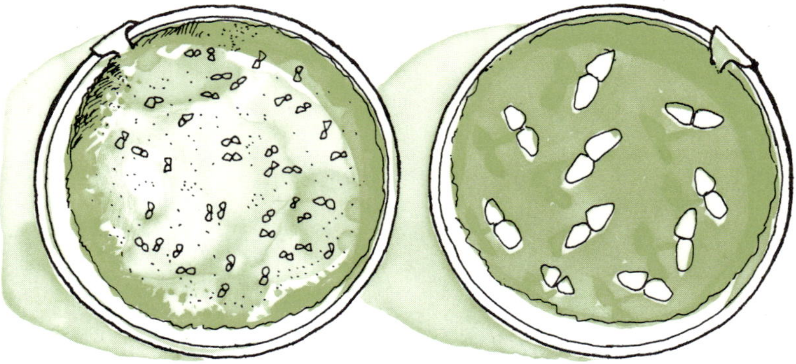

By taking care simply to space out any seeds large enough to handle and to mix tiny seeds with sand the seedlings have plenty of room to develop from the moment they appear. It makes pricking out easier, too.

dibber is then used to make a hole for the young plant which is settled with its seed leaves only just above soil level.

When pricking out seedlings, set them deep enough for the seed leaves to just sit on the surface of the compost.

A slightly different technique is easier for larger seedlings. After covering the drainage layer with about 1 inch (2 cm) of lightly-firmed compost put a little more of the medium into the pot and draw it to one side with your fingers. Hold the seedling in position with its roots spread out over this compost, then trickle in more to fill the space left and gently firm it. A final rap of the pot on the bench will level any loose compost. It takes a little practice to get the amount of compost right for each stage, but it is not long before you will be able to pot off seedlings quickly to leave them placed centrally and at the right depth. There should be ½ in (1 cm) of space between soil and pot rim to contain water when it is given.

Moving seedlings into a larger size of pot is called 'potting-on'. The new pot should usually allow about an inch (2 cm) of space around the ball of roots and old compost. Pots of the 5 in (12.5 cm) size are the most useful. Having arranged any necessary drainage layer, cover this with a 1 inch (2 cm) layer of firmed compost and stand the plant in place, after removing any crocks or other drainage material from the base of its soil ball. Adjust the quantity of compost in the bottom of the new pot, if necessary, so that the top of the old soil ball will finish at about ¾ in (1.5 cm) below the rim of the new container, again to allow for watering. Then trickle fresh compost in around the roots and press it firm.

When potting on always remember to water the plants a few hours

Vigorous growing seedlings, such as those of tomatoes and capsicums, need plenty of root room and should be moved directly into small pots.

beforehand to ensure that the old ball of roots and soil will be moist. Also aim to make the new compost just firmer than the old. If this is not done any water tends to drain mainly through the new compost leaving the roots and old compost dry. Provided the plants are first watered and the new compost is moist there is no need to water plants immediately after such a move when using a soil-based compost. In fact it pays to keep the plants rather on the dry side for a few days after potting on since this encourages their roots to explore the new soil more quickly. If the weather is sunny they may need to be lightly shaded and syringed with water to help prevent them flagging, but on no account allow the compost to dry out completely.

If you use J I composts, use No 1 when potting off and No 2 for all but slow-growing plants. With a peat-based medium use potting compost for both, but again,take care not to over compress it. Only the lightest finger pressure is needed for the first potting. And being much better aerated than soil-based composts, peat ones are best kept watered. If allowed to dry out they are much more difficult to rewet.

When to Move

The time to move seedlings on into larger pots is judged by their root development, and this can be seen if a plant is tapped out of its pot.

Slide one hand across the top of the pot so that the plant stem lies between your fingers, then invert the pot and tap the rim on the greenhouse bench or a tool handle to loosen it. The pot can then be lifted off to expose the ball of soil and roots.

If the outer part of the soil ball is well netted with roots it is time the young plant had a larger pot. If the roots have run around the outer base of the ball to form a thick 'rope', it has already been left too long in the small pot and is becoming root-bound. These guide lines apply only to seedlings, however. Once a plant is in it final pot size it will naturally fill it with roots. Indeed, many plants only flower well when they reach a root-bound condition.

Provided you use clean containers and compost and grow your plants in hygienic conditions you will avoid most seedling diseases - especially 'damping-off', which took an enormous toll of seedlings

When large seeds such as marrows are sown two to a pot, remove the weaker soon after germination if both seeds grow.

before modern seed composts were introduced. Symptom of the trouble was a shrivelling of the stems at soil level that caused the seedlings to topple over. Should damping-off occur, water the containers as soon as possible with Cheshunt Compound.

Once the containers are sown and covered, germination takes place in a closed environment. From the time the seedlings appear and are uncovered they are subject to the general conditions of the greenhouse or frame in which they are growing and this environment must be adapted to suit them. They will also need to be watered whenever the soil dries.

Watering Technique

Watering is, perhaps, the most misunderstood and mismanaged aspect of growing plants in containers. The trouble is that it cannot be done efficiently by any precise timing method or rota system. The type of plant, and its development, as well as temperature and atmospheric humidity, all have a bearing on how quickly it takes up moisture, while the material from which the pot is made, the type of compost - even the degree to which it is compressed - can affect the amount of water held in reserve. With very few exceptions plants do

A long-spouted Haws' pattern can is best for watering pots and boxes. Turn the fine rose upwards to get a gentle spray.

not like their roots in soggy, poorly aerated soil, yet this is in effect what they get if overwatered. And because seedlings take up very little water at first they are much more likely to be overwatered than large plants.

The first step to watering control actually comes when preparing trays and pots for sowing by making sure that they can drain freely. As previously explained this is done by putting a layer of drainage material in the base of containers to be filled with a soil compost and ensuring that the compost, especially a peat one, is not over-firmed. There should be a space left between the surface of the compost and container rim to hold water when applying it.

Overwatering does not mean giving too much water at one time,because if the drainage is adequate surplus water will quickly drain away to let air in. But rather it is a matter of giving water too often. When watering enough must be given to wet the whole ball of roots and soil by filling the container to the brim and allowing it to percolate through, and giving yet more if this is not enough. Ideally, a pot should shed a drop or two of water from the base after watering to show it has had enough. If too much water is given it will drain out in a puddle, taking plant foods with it. Then, having watered the container thoroughly, allow time for the soil to become rather dry before watering it again. You can usually assess the dryness of plastic pots filled with peat compost by their weight and that of soil compost by the dryness at the surface. Alternatively you can use an inexpensive electronic meter with a probe to measure the moisture content.

Should the containers be allowed to become too dry they are difficult to rewet by ordinary means. Instead the best way is to stand them in a tray filled with water deep enough to reach almost level with the surface of the soil in the pots or trays that are dry and allow them to soak for a few minutes until the moisture reaches the top of the soil, then leave them to drain.

Although plants in containers can be fed with dry fertilisers, it is best to dissolve the food into the water that is given to them. In any case, provided seedlings are properly looked after as they develop, being pricked out or potted off and planted out or potted on promptly, they are unlikely to need any supplementary feeding until they have been in their final pots or open ground for some weeks.

Growing Desert Cacti

Desert cacti are a group that call for rather different treatment to most other seedlings, but before dealing with their special needs one or two misconceptions about these plants should be cleared up. To begin with not all cacti are desert types. Some, mostly the epiphytic ones, like the Easter cactus (*rhipsalidopsis*), the Christmas cactus (*shlumbergera*) and orchid cactus (*epiphyllum*) come from a completely different environment and should never be allowed to suffer from drought. Indeed the compost they are growing in should never be

1. For most developing plants a pot 1-1½ in (2-3 cm) wider than the existing one is needed when potting on. Firm sufficient fresh compost into the base to support the plant at the correct height.

2. To remove the old pot, slide your hand across the top so that the stem sits between your fingers, then invert the plant, tap the pot rim against the bench or tool to loosen it and lift it off.

allowed to become anywhere near dry. These varieties can be raised from seed quite easily and grown on using normal techniques. Do not cover the seeds after sowing them, but when the seedlings appear the young plants should be shaded from strong direct sunlight in spring and summer.

The true desert cacti can stand a great deal of drought, but that is

3. Stand the plant centrally in its new pot, then trickle fresh compost in around its roots, firming it in layers as you go. It should finish level with or just cover the top of the old root ball.

4. You are less likely to over-compress the new compost, especially a peat-based one if you use your fingers when pressing down. It should be made slightly firmer than the old compost.

not to say they should have to. Indeed many are stunted by not having enough water. Only during their resting period, which is usually during winter, should they be kept dry and water given only when they show signs of shrivelling. As the growing season begins, increase the frequency of watering and during summer rewet the compost as soon as it becomes quite dry. Also feed the plants regularly at this time. At the end of the growing period again reduce the watering until they are left dry once again. If not supplied with food and water at the correct time desert cacti are unable to grow properly and can neither develop into handsome specimens nor flower, in the case of those that will do so in this country.

One thing these plants cannot abide is a permanently soggy compost. Always pay special attention to the drainage, therefore, and use a compost with a really open texture. You can buy special potting compost for desert cacti, or make it yourself by adding one part of coarse sand or sterilised (baked) crushed brick to two parts of J I potting compost No 1. When watering plants during their growth period, give enough to wet the whole potful of soil, just as you would for any other plant. But then wait until the soil is quite dry before watering again. If the roots of desert cacti are kept wet for long they soon rot.

Seeds of cacti vary in size from dust-like to large, and should be sown on the surface of the compost. Ordinary peat-based composts seem to work well, but some experts prefer to use J I sowing compost and add a third part by bulk of coarse sand. The large seeds are easily spaced out individually and just pressed into the soil surface. The small ones have to be scattered, preferably after being mixed with a little clean, fine sand to help get an even distribution. Put the containers into plastic bags to help keep them moist until the seedlings appear, which usually takes 2-4 weeks. Desert cacti do not need a very high germinating temperature: indeed many come from

Using a rose when watering pots, even large ones, saves disturbing or washing out the compost.

areas where the nights can be decidedly cold. Most germinate well when kept at 55-60F (13-16C).

When the seedlings appear shade them from strong sunlight. If you do not they may turn red in colour and slow down their development - even stop growing - for the rest of the season. The quickest growing species will probably be large enough to prick out or pot out during the first summer, but provided the seeds were well spaced out they can be left in the seed containers until the following spring. The size they reach depends in part on the sowing date and the earlier they are started off the better. The larger they are at the end of the summer, the easier it is to get them through the first winter. Being small they cannot hold a great reserve of moisture and tend to desiccate, hence they need to be watered more often. When kept in a barely heated greenhouse, therefore, they may succumb to excessive dampness. It is best if they are kept to a minimum temperature of 60F (16C) and kept growing until the second resting period arrives. By then they should be sizeable specimens and fit in with your routine for looking after the others.

Although I have singled out desert cacti for this type of treatment, it also suits many other exotic succulent plants that come from the drier regions of the world.

Hardening Off Young Plants

All plants that are to be raised under glass before being set out in the open, be they vegetable or flower seedlings, must be given a period of

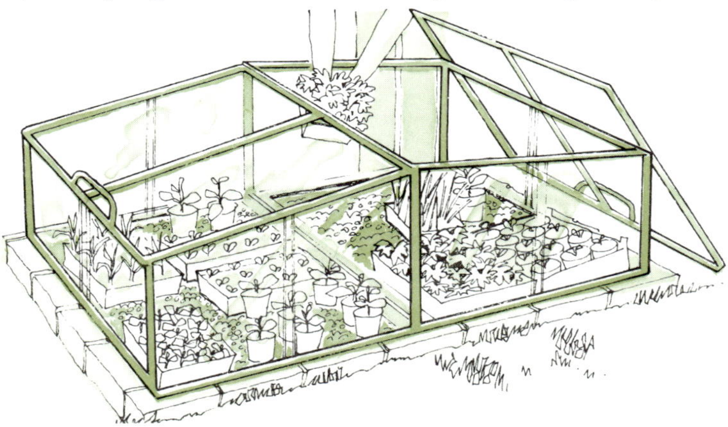

Apart from its use for raising hardy plants from seed, a cold frame is an indispensible adjunct to a greenhouse when raising half-hardy plants to set outdoors. These must receive a period of acclimatisation before being planted in the open ground.

acclimatisation, or hardening-off. The sudden change from indoor to outdoor conditions would be too much of a shock. At best the plants would receive a severe setback to their growth; at worst their soft tissues could suffer weather damage and they could possibly die. The necessary acclimatisation is best given in a cold frame where the seedlings can be given increasing ventilation over a period of two or three weeks until the frame light can be left off altogether day and night, unless a frost or heavy rain is likely. Take special care to see that they do not suffer from lack of water. As ventilation is increased following removal of the frame light, the seedlings will lose moisture more quickly through their leaves in the drier air and pots and boxes will need to be watered more often.

During the period of hardening-off, the plant tissues will become tougher and usually turn a darker green. If they show signs of developing a bluish tinge, however, you are doing the job too quickly, since the bluish colour is usually the result of seedlings feeling cold. And do not neglect to feed those plants that need it - or you can get other colours appearing as well.

Preparation for Planting Out

While the plants are being acclimatised, the area where they are to be planted out should be prepared ready for them by breaking it up, working in any fertiliser, manure or peat needed, then treading it down and raking the top level. There is no need to create as fine a tilth as you would for seed sowing, but a loose, reasonably fine surface layer makes the work of hoeing and weeding easier later on.

A day or two before planting, check how moist the soil is and give it a thorough watering if it is dry. This will give time for the surplus water to drain away from the surface and leave it in a fit condition for planting. Such watering not only ensures that the young plants start off with a full reserve of moisture in the soil, but also that surface evaporation will keep up the humidity around them and help them recover from any root disturbance.

At planting time use a garden line and a measuring rod - a 5-6 ft (1.5-1.75 m) long batten - marked in feet and inches, or metres and centimetres if you have 'gone metric' - when setting out in rows to get the plants properly positioned. It is quicker simply to stand each plant in its correct position along a row first, then return to carry out the job of actually planting them in the soil. If two people can work as a team, one siting the plants while the other sets them in the soil, it takes less than half the time when a large number of seedlings is being dealt with.

When arranging plants in a bed for display, it pays to mark out the

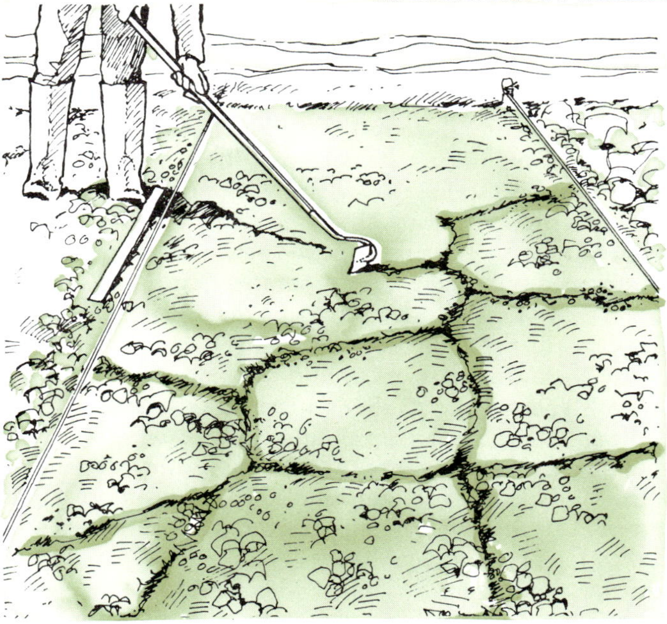

Mark out the areas where each plant is to grow before beginning to sow a border of mixed annuals.

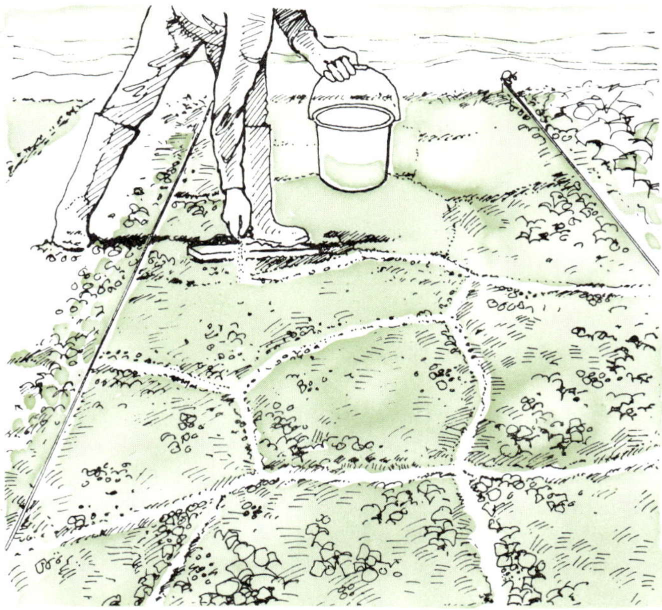

If it is difficult to see the marks when the soil dries out, scatter a little sand along them.

site first by drawing out shallow drills to form a grid on the soil surface, using a line as a guide and adjusting the distances according to the type of plant. All you then need to do is to put out each group of plants in turn, setting them out where the lines intersect. A circular bed can be marked in rings by a loop of string with a peg at the end running from a central stake.

When spacing out the seedlings, those in pots can be stood out where they are, the pot being removed at the time of planting. Those growing in seed trays have to be separated first. This is best done by running a sharp knife along and across the tray between the rows of seedlings to cut through their roots. Each can then be lifted out separately with a cube of roots and soil which is their fair share, otherwise if you try to pull them apart inevitably some have more than others. All the containers should be thoroughly watered a short time before planting to ensure that the plants are fully charged with moisture. Provided this is done, most plants will hardly notice the move and even those separated up from trays suffer little check to growth.

Make the planting holes with the aid of a trowel and aim to set the plants so that the top of the block of roots and soil is level with or just below the surface when the loosened soil is pressed firm around them. You can judge the depth for those in pots by standing them pot-and-all in the hole first then make any necessary adjustments before removing the container. This is done by placing one hand across the rim, with the plant between your fingers then inverting the pot and rapping the rim or base with a trowel to loosen it. The pot can then be lifted off and, if it is a clay pot, any drainage crocks removed from the base of the root ball before the plant is placed in its allotted hole. Those plants raised in peat or Fyba pots can, of course, be planted pot and all.

Firm the Soil

Once each plant is set in place, firm the soil tightly about it. You can tread around those from larger pots, but to avoid damage it is safer to ram the soil down with your trowel handle or press it tightly around their roots with your knuckles, when planting seedlings from small pots and boxes. Such firming is essential, indeed it is the essence of good planting and the quick establishment of young plants. A sure test is to hold a leaf of a plant between finger and thumb and pull. If the leaf tears across all is well, but if the plant is pulled up the soil was not pressed firmly enough about its roots.

This firming of the soil serves three important functions. It prevents rapid evaporation of soil moisture, which occurs when the

When moving young plants into larger pots, the top of the root ball should be just covered and sufficient space left between compost and pot rim to hold water when it is given.

After being planted in open ground and the soil firmed about them, the ball of roots and soil of each seedling should finish just below the surface of the soil.

surface is too loose, it encourages the rapid development of new roots which must have intimate contact with the soil, and it gives a plant support and helps to keep it upright.

Once all the plants have been set out, water them in by pouring about half a pint (30 cl) of water around the base of each. This helps to settle the soil more firmly and destroys any hidden air pockets beneath the surface. When setting out brassicas, follow the watering in by applying a suitable soil insecticide around the plants to ward off root fly attacks. Finish the job by hoeing the area to loosen the surface, erase footprints and leave it looking tidy. And if your garden is slug-ridden, do remember to scatter bait over newly planted areas to deal with these pests, especially if the seedlings are on the small side. Nothing is more annoying than to have to fill in any gaps a week later, or frustrating if you have no spare plants with which to fill the gaps.

Provided the ground was moist to begin with, the containers were watered beforehand and the plants set at the right depth and properly firmed in, they should quickly settle down and grow away. From that time on they come under your general garden routine for watering, feeding and spraying. There is no doubt that starting with high quality plants is the first step towards getting the best results. And provided you are prepared to give them proper attention there is no reason why your seedlings should not be as good, and can frequently be better, than those that are sold in shops and garden centres.

It is not really difficult to meet the needs of seedlings; the real art, if it can be so called, in raising good plants is tending to their needs in good time. They must be kept moving steadily from the time they germinate without suffering from drought, starvation, root constriction or lack of space. Then they are full of vitality and have the ability to be lavish in their flowering or cropping power.

Keep a Record

A mistake usually made by people new to plant raising indoors is the failure to get the necessary materials in hand in good time. It is no good waiting until plants need more space before finding you have not enough pots or compost. Or to wait until plants show signs of starvation before realising you have no suitable food for them. An adequate stock must be ready for use when required.

Another common error, due to lack of experience, is to sow too many different seeds at once with the result that the seedlings all need

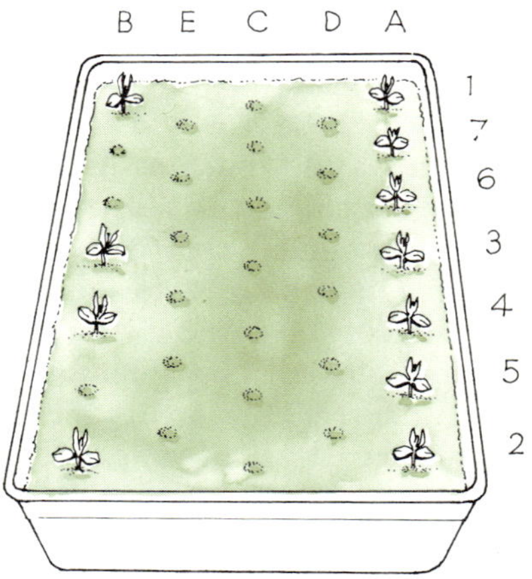

Suggested sequence for pricking out so that the seedlings are evenly spaced. Start with row A, setting the end seedlings first, then the middle one; followed by others are indicated by numbers. Procede to row B, and so on.

to be pricked out or potted off at the same time. If you are raising only a moderate number of plants this may not matter, but if you are organising a large bedding display it can be quite a headache. None of us has unlimited time at our disposal.

This is one reason why keeping a few records can be invaluable. If you jot down sowing, pricking-out and potting-on dates for the various plants you can refer to them another year when working out your sowing schedule. A note of the stage of seedlings at planting out time can also be valuable, as can a note of the time flowering or cropping commenced. Some may be better sown earlier or later to forward or retard their development. I think it is better to err on the side of late sowing, rather than be too early in the spring until you gain experience. A delayed crop or display can be a disappointment, but this is better than the embarrassment that can occur if frost-tender plants are ready for setting out before it is safe to do so. Some form of garden record, no matter how simple, can be invaluable when making future plans.

Pests and Diseases

Provided you pay attention to keeping the structure clean and tidy and use clean containers and sterilised composts there are not many pests and diseases that are likely to prove troublesome to seedlings in a greenhouse used primarily for raising plants. But when it is shared with a mixed collection of plants, and especially where it is heated throughout the winter, there is always a source of possible infection or infestation at hand.

Aphides are ubiquitous in all their many forms and are as commonly met with under glass as outside. There are plenty of efficient modern sprays that can be used to control them. The only other serious common pest is red spider mite. This tiny creature is hardly visible to the naked eye, and it is the symptoms rather than the pest that are first seen. They cause a yellow or whitish mottling of the leaves and stems which, in a severe attack, become almost entirely yellow and covered in a fine web. This pest flourishes where the air is hot and dry. Consequently, its worst attacks usually develop in summer.

The first obvious step in the control of red spider mite is to keep up the atmospheric humidity. There are sprays, too, that can be used to help control it, though efficient spraying is difficult to achieve in a small garden greenhouse.

Woodlice, though not usually particularly troublesome pests, can become destructive in old greenhouses and frames, especially wooden ones. Piles of dirty boxes and pots and other rubbish or litter also provide homes for them. These creatures attack small seedlings, and eat through their stems. The answer is again to practise sensible hygiene to begin with. Then if they are still a problem dust corners and other likely hiding places with a suitable insecticidal dust.

Mice can be a nuisance in some greenhouses and frames not only damaging seedlings but removing seeds as well. A few strategically placed break-back traps is usually the answer. The metal, so-called self-setting traps are easier to use than the old wooden design. You may find you have to experiment with bait to catch them, however. The most likely ones are bread crust, cheese rind (especially if frizzled with a match) and, as a last resort, chocolate. But do make sure that pets and birds cannot be accidentally caught in the traps.

Where you have a lot of pots sown with seed in a cold frame or plunge bed where they will be left perhaps for months, it pays to cover them with fine mesh wire netting to keep off mice and birds.

Apart from damping off diseases, which attack young seedlings, but which should never trouble you if you use clean containers and sterilised composts, the only general disease which may prove troublesome to young plants under glass is grey mould, also known as

As seedlings increase in size, so does their need for watering which must be regularly attended to. A long-spouted Haws' can is invaluable when using a wide, or high-sided frame, enabling you to reach the centre comfortably from either side.

botrytis. This can be very troublesome where plants stay wet for long periods and it also readily invades any damaged or dying tissues. The first step in its control is to ensure adequate ventilation to prevent build-up of excess humidity, which can condense out on plants when the temperature falls, and to take care not to splash water about at times when it is too cold to ventilate the structure freely. Secondly, never leave fallen leaves, faded flowers or other odds and ends of plant material lying about. And if despite your efforts you find conditions developing that will encourage it, or the first signs of its grey, fluffy mould, use a suitable chemical aid to combat it.

Using a liquid spray for the control of botrytis can be self-defeating in muggy weather unless you can apply it very thoroughly indeed. At such times it is probably better to use a fumigant. Certainly these are highly effective in a greenhouse which can be closed to contain the vapours.

Greenhouse Smokes

A number of fumigants is available to deal with a variety of pests and diseases. They are available as pellets or smoke cones which, once ignited, produce a pungent smoke that penetrates every nook and cranny throughout the whole greenhouse and coats everything with the chemical it carries. The job is best done on a still evening when the ventilators and door can be closed for the night. The air should be reasonably still because it is amazing how many air gaps there actually are in a greenhouse through which smoke can escape, and if there is anything approaching a breeze the smoke may disperse before it has had a chance to do what is required. When used correctly greenhouse smokes are one of the most effective, and certainly the easiest, ways of controlling pests and diseases under glass.

I must, however, add a word of warning. Do read the small print on any spray container or smoke cone to make sure it is safe to use on all the plants you have in your greenhouse. There are a few plants that are highly allergic to various chemicals and easily damaged or killed by them, even if not sprayed directly. And if you use a smoke generator, leave the greenhouse closed and locked for the night. Then ventilate it freely the following day before working inside it. In other words do read and follow the manufacturer's directions for every product.

6. Tools and Equipment

1. For Sowing Outdoors

There is a great number of tools and items of equipment available to home gardeners to help with seedling raising. But before rushing out to buy them it pays to consider how useful they really are. While many of the products can speed work or increase your chances of success, you must have a real need for any item in order for it to be worthy of investment, and that depends on your style of gardening and the plants you intend to raise.

The basic tool kit for outdoor plant raising should consist of a spade, digging fork, rake, line and reel, draw hoe, Dutch hoe, trowel and hand fork, and a watering can. All are available in a variety of shapes and sizes and made of different materials. Some people prefer one type, others another. But for the benefit of any beginner I shall state my own preferences and reasons.

Choosing a Spade

A spade is the basic garden digging tool and is used for a great deal of hard work. I much prefer the type that does not have a flat tread on top of the blade. Although this makes for heavy wear on your boots, the soil cannot clog at the top of the blade as it does under a tread - especially on heavy ground - and so increase your work load. It also makes cleaning the spade with a scraper easier and quicker. I have had two expensive spades made of stainless steel, but now-a-days use one with an ordinary steel blade, which I find stays sharper longer and that also reduces effort required.

Incidentally, a spade scraper is invaluable when digging. Mine is made from a piece of copper pipe partly sawn through on one side to allow the end to be opened out and hammered flat to form a scraping blade.

For spring and summer digging, when the soil needs to be broken up fine, a fork is the better tool. It is useful also to mix in fertiliser dressings, loosen the surface and for rough raking. Whilst a stainless steel fork is better looking, I cannot say that it is more efficient than a steel one, provided you wipe it clean after use.

Although it is possible to use two stout sticks and a length of string as a line when marking out rows, you will find it saves both time and temper if you have a stout nylon line that does not easily break, even when accidentally chopped with a spade. It is much more convenient, too, to have a peg and reel for the line, so that it can be pulled taut and securely anchored in place when in use, yet easily wound up again afterwards. There is no need for the spikes on peg and reel to be very large - mine are about 9 in (23 cm) long and perfectly satisfactory. Excessive length of the spikes means more work to push them into the ground, especially if it is stony, and pull them up again.

Different Hoes

A draw hoe is the handiest tool for taking out seed drills. Easiest of all to use is the swan-necked pattern where the blade is held several

This is my basic tool kit for raising plants from seed out of doors. Hanging from left to right are a line and reel, weeding fork, Dutch hoe, trowel, digging spade and fork, rake and draw hoe. Below are a plastic bucket and watering can. These can be augmented later with other tools, such as a border fork, onion hoe and tined cultivator, if the need arises.

inches beyond the handle by a curved shank (see page 108). These tools tend to deteriorate more due to rusting than wear and it is worth obtaining one made of stainless steel where possible. I bought mine many years ago and it is still going strong.

The best tool for controlling weeds between rows of tiny seedlings is still a Dutch hoe. Used with a pushing motion it can be used to skim just under the soil close to tiny seedlings without heaping soil over them. When the seedlings grow larger one of the modern push-pull hoes can be used instead. These enable you to cover the ground faster when the surface is sufficiently dry, but a Dutch hoe will still make a better job of it if the soil tends to cling.

A garden trowel is invaluable when moving plants, not only for excavating the holes for them, but also for lifting seedlings with a good block of soil about their roots. Having a curved blade, two or three nearly vertical cuts around the plants releases a tapering cylinder of earth that is easily lifted out. This is another tool where stainless steel really is worth the extra expense. But do not buy the cheapest; choose one that is cast or forged from solid metal. Those formed by pressing thin sheet to shape soon bend and become virtually worthless, especially if your soil is on the heavy side. To go with your trowel a hand weeding fork can also be useful for lifting seedlings when transplanting, especially where they are too close together in the rows to be lifted individually. Again, go for strength - cheap hand forks soon bend out of shape.

Watering Cans

The final item on my list of basic tools is a watering can. There is hardly a time when young plants are not better for being watered in immediately after being transplanted. A quick flush of water directed about them destroys any hidden air pockets and settles the soil in intimate contact with their roots. I also use mine a great deal in the summer for flooding seed drills just before sowing seeds to secure quick and certain germination. Equipped with a rose it is useful too, for keeping rows of tiny plants moist in dry weather. The 2-gallon (9-litre) size is probably the most useful, holding a respectable quantity of water yet not too heavy when full. And if your garden is more than pocket-hankerchief size a pair of matching cans makes for comfort when carrying water any distance, because one balances the other.

The basic tool kit is usually expanded over the years as the need for various tools develops. A tined cultivator, for instance, is useful for breaking down winter-dug ground in spring and mixing fertiliser into the soil. An onion hoe - a short swan-necked hoe that is held in one hand - though usually bought for hoeing around close-set plants, is less unwieldy to use than a full-sized one when drawing a series of short drills in a seedbed. A border fork, which is a lighter, smaller version of a digging fork, is handy for lifting larger plants, such as wallflowers that are being moved into their final, flowering quarters in autumn. It is better to wait until a real need arises before investing in special purpose tools, as they are hardly worth buying for raising plants from seeds alone.

Mechanical Cultivators

Sooner or later a gardener with a large vegetable plot will consider whether he could not ease his work load by using a mechanical cultivator to break up the ground and save the laborious job of hand-digging. The answer is that you can, but the results are never as good as when the area is turned over rough in the autumn with a spade and exposed to winter weathering, especially on heavy ground. The trouble is that these machines break up the soil too finely for efficient weathering, since it is easily beaten flat again by winter rains. If a machine is used for autumn digging it should be fitted with a ridging attachment. By throwing up the soil in ridges there is more chance for winter frosts to do their beneficial work. Next to spade work, ploughing is best and a mechanical cultivator comes a poor third in winter digging.

Where these machines do come into their own, however, is in preparing ground for immediate sowing and planting. It may be that you are starting a garden from scratch, or breaking up an area you did not have time to dig. Under these circumstances a mechanical cultivator is much speedier and more efficient than forking by hand. The same applies when the finished winter greens crops are cleared in the spring or, indeed, when preparing any ground after any crop that is to be followed immediately by another.

Watering Equipment

Efficient watering is one of the keys to raising plants from seed successfully out of doors in the summer. Dryness can delay plant development, even result in the death of young seedlings in extreme cases. A hosepipe and an efficient sprinkler are invaluable therefore. For watering young seedlings and areas sown with seeds a sprinkler that applies water as a misty spray is best. With its aid sufficient water can be applied to saturate the top 12 in (30 cm) of soil without either 'panning' the surface or splattering tiny seedlings with mud. Because watering in this way does not spoil the soil texture or puddle the surface it is ideal, too, for re-wetting an area cleared of a crop in spring or summer before preparing it for the next. The only drawback with this type of sprinkler is that it needs to be moved fairly frequently, usually every 20-30 minutes, depending on the dryness and type of the soil. But considered purely from the point of view of watering it is by far the most efficient for seedlings. When the plants are about 6 in (15 cm) high, an oscillating sprinkler, which applies water in larger drops over a much larger area, can be more convenient.

Cloches Speed Growth

Cloches can be invaluable aids to most gardeners and I have already described the advantages of using them to enable earlier sowing to be made outdoors and forward the growth of young seedlings. There are many patterns available, but they can be broadly divided into two groups according to whether they are glazed with glass or made with plastic. Glass cloches are more efficient at trapping heat and the most dependable for protecting tender plants and really early crops. Against this must be set the fact that they are heavy to move and that the glass is easily broken. Plastic ones, even those made from clear polythene, are surprisingly effective. Cheapest to buy are polythene tunnel cloches, which consist of a long length of plastic sheeting held over wire hoops, but they are not easily moved. Possibly the best all-round cloches are those made from Novolux corrugated vinyl sheet held in galvanised metal frames. They are easy to move or take apart to store flat when not required.

Though not essential, a soil thermometer is extremely useful, especially when used in conjunction with cloches. With its aid you can assess when extra early sowings are likely to get away to a good start. Having put your cloches in place to warm up the soil, by using a soil thermometer you can keep a check on its temperature. As soon as this registers 45F (7C) you can put in sowings of most hardy crops and hardy annuals with every expectation of getting successful germination. Tender crops like dwarf and runner beans, and sweet corn can be sown when the soil temperature reading reaches 55F (13C) provided the plants will not need to be uncovered before risk of late frost is past, but wait until the thermometer registers 60F(16C) before putting in marrows and cucumbers. A soil thermometer is an extremely valuable aid in making the earliest possible sowings a real success.

2. For plant raising under glass

A garden greenhouse is the largest investment most people make in their gardens. It opens up a whole new realm of gardening opportunities and is most valuable to anyone who aspires to raise a wide range of plants from seed, though the main reason why many gardeners buy a greenhouse is often to grow their own tomatoes, chrysanthemums or some other special crop.

Greenhouses come in a diversity of shapes, sizes and materials. My present one has an aluminium structure and I would not choose any other. They come in pieces and assembling them is a fiddly business, but once erected an aluminium model is all but maintenance free, which is more than can be said for any timber structure. Although there are greenhouses available that are covered with plastic, they have a limited usefulness and durability. If you intend to make full use of your greenhouse and want to heat it in order to raise tender plants from seed it is sensible to choose one which has glass panels.

Glass-to-ground Greenhouse

The most versatile greenhouse design for garden use is one that is glazed to ground level. This can be fitted with benches, or staging, early in the year when raising plants from seed. Later this staging can be removed from either or both sides to make room for tall-growing crops such as tomatoes and cucumbers. Where a greenhouse is to be used mainly for raising plants and heated at least during the early months of the year, a structure with solid sides up to staging level would be more economical to run.

What size of greenhouse to buy is a problem to decide and to some extent depends on the space available, cost and the use to which it is to be put. My advice is to buy one larger than you think you need because it is amazing how quickly its space is filled as your interests grow. Besides, the larger it is the easier it is to control the environment within it. And it is for this reason also that you should have one fitted with plenty of ventilators. The ventilation of so-called 'standard' models with only one ventilator in the roof and one in the side is generally hopelessly inadequate, unless fitted with an extractor fan for automatic ventilation.

A greenhouse can be constructed on foundations that allow plants to be grown in soil beds within the structure. Alternatively it can be erected on a solid base of concrete. For a propagation house the latter is best since it can be kept clean and is easily disinfected when necessary. I prefer it in any case to a soil bed even where summer crops are grown, since they can be set out in growing-bags to ensure a really clean start. Soil beds can be difficult to water, become infected with diseases and the soil becomes 'sick' when the same crop is grown in it again and again. Weeds too can be a perennial nuisance in soil beds. I would not consider having soil beds in a greenhouse unless I intended to grow permanent subjects such as tender shrubs or fruit, peaches or apricots for instance.

Need for a Frame

As well as a greenhouse you need a garden frame, because a frame is virtually a necessary extension of a greenhouse when raising plants from seed, quite apart from being better than a greenhouse in some circumstances. A large part of the output from a greenhouse is usually frost-tender plants, such as half-hardy annual flowers and summer crops like marrows, cucumbers and sweet corn. These appreciate the extra warmth provided by a greenhouse during the first 6-8 weeks of their lives, but need to be acclimatised to outdoor conditions before being planted in the garden. Such 'hardening-off', as it is called is best accomplished in a frame where the plants can gradually be given more air until the top, or frame light, can be left off altogether, being replaced only if heavy rain or frost is likely.

The ability to move seedlings into a frame allows the greenhouse space to be given over to the plants that really need it. And during the summer months many greenhouse plants can be housed happily in a frame to make space for tomatoes and other summer crops. Early in the year a frame can be the best place for sowings for hardy plants that do not need, and are often better without, high temperature in order to germinate, especially those seeds that need a dose of winter cold. It is also the best place for seedlings like cinerarias and greenhouse primulas which, although they need frost protection in the winter, do appreciate cool conditions in the summer.

Ideally two frames are needed: first is a capacious, glass-to-ground model that can be used for hardening off half-hardy plants to be set outdoors and for growing tender plants in the summer. Second is a smaller substantially-sided type that can be filled with peat or sand to act as a plunge bed in which pots can be sunk to the rim. This is the best way to deal with sowings of hardy plants and shrubs that need a period of cold to trigger germination. The pots are exposed to frost and snow, the glazed light only being used to protect them from heavy rain that might disturb the seeds or seedlings. It is also a good place to germinate in the spring those hardy plants without inhibited germination if the seeds are too small or expensive to be risked in the open garden.

Heating Systems

A basic greenhouse fitted with staging, together with a frame, offers great scope for anyone who wants to raise plants from seed. Even greenhouse plants that need a high germinating temperature can be attempted successfully in the summer. For the greatest flexibility and opportunity, however, some form of heating is needed to maintain a minimum temperature of 50F (10C) in the greenhouse, or part of it, from the beginning of March. This will enable a timely start to be made with such summer bedding plants as lobelia, fibrous-rooted begonias and salvias that take the longest time to reach flowering size. Although they ideally should be kept at a minimum temperature of 60F (16C) they will survive night temperatures a little lower after they have been pricked out. For the initial stages of germination they can be kept in a heated propagator, that I shall deal with later.

A greenhouse can be heated by means of solid fuel or oil-burning boilers supplying hot water pipes, paraffin heaters, gas heaters or electricity. Each method has its advantages and drawbacks. The prices of fuels have fluctuated over the years and one cannot be sure that the system chosen today will necessarily be the most economical to run in the future.

In terms of cost for heat generated, solid fuel is the leader. The method of combustion involves losses, however, and the fact that the system is not flexible in operation means that more heat is wasted. A large amount of water has to be heated up and this continues to dissipate its heat long after the need for it has passed. So although modern boilers have some form of thermostatic control to maintain a certain water temperature, this has little relation to actual greenhouse temperature. Solid fuel heating systems are expensive to buy and need regular attention. You also need somewhere nearby to store the fuel. But where the heat requirement is large and fairly constant, as it is in winter for instance, there is much to recommend a solid-fuel heating system. It also has an advantage of having no electric controls and is therefore not subject to breakdown due to power failures, which always seem to occur at the most inopportune times.

Gas heating, where available, can be used either to heat water in a boiler or to provide direct hot-air heating within the greenhouse, which is more efficient. It can be cheaper to operate than electric heating, but needs to be controlled electrically via a thermostat to prevent wastage. Installation costs of a mains supply can be heavy if the greenhouse is sited far from an existing supply point,although it is possible to use butane gas in cylinders.

Paraffin blue-flame heaters are relatively cheap to buy and reasonably economical to operate, but they do need regular attention by way of filling and cleaning. If more than one burner is used the heat output can be cut if required by lighting only as many as you estimate will be needed to maintain a sufficiently high temperature. Sited within a greenhouse, both paraffin and gas heaters must have an adequate supply of air in order to burn properly. Without sufficient oxygen they emit toxic fumes that can be harmful to plants - and you. The extra ventilation needed does, of course, increase heat losses and so reduces their efficiency.

Electricity provides the most expensive form of heating, but it is also the most flexible, clean and trouble-free source. With the use of an efficient fan heater and an accurate rod thermostat set at plant level, heat wastage can be cut to a minimum. Due to the losses incurred with other heating systems, the comparative costs of the various heating fuels in terms of British Thermal Units can be misleading, making electricity seem more expensive than it really is. The major cost of installing the system involves laying on the electricity to the greenhouse, which, for safety's sake, must be done by a competent electrician. It would be unfair to charge the whole amount to heating, since a power supply is useful for many other purposes too. Once installed, electricity certainly wins on convenience. It can be turned on at the flick of a switch or automatic time switch, needs practically no maintenance and, with proper controls, can safely be left to get on with the job for weeks at a time if necessary - though it does leave you at the mercy of supply breakdowns and power cuts.

Two-system Economy

The most economical method of heating a large garden greenhouse to a minimum temperature is to use two systems, utilising solid fuel to supply the bulk of your requirements together with an electric fan heater that will cut in to act as a booster only when extreme conditions bring about extra low temperatures. In this way you will enjoy the best advantages of both - cheaper costs for the bulk of your heating, but flexibility to meet unusual demands. Regular attention is called for, but you still have one source of heating available should the other fail for any reason.

Perhaps I am old-fashioned, but I do not believe a better method of greenhouse heating has been evolved than that which uses large water pipes running the length of the greenhouse and heated by a boiler. The heat is well spread and the rising warm air sets up gentle currents that prevent pockets of stagnant air developing to encourage diseases. It is also a dry heat, adding no extra moisture to the atmosphere in winter when excessive humidity can be a problem. The nearest equivalent is electrical tubular heaters. Electric fan heaters are effective, too, for providing that essential air movement. The drawback of burning paraffin and gas in a greenhouse is that they both load the air with extra moisture. And unless such heaters are provided with some method of distributing their warmth, air circulation can be erratic, even non-existent in the corners of a structure which are then not only colder, but often the point where diseases first strike.

Heat Conservation

In order to keep greenhouse heating costs to an acceptable level you must as far as possible prevent waste. Due to their method and materials of construction most greenhouses tend to lose heat readily. As a first stage, therefore, do keep the structure in good repair. Cracked and broken panes of glass should be replaced and the woodwork kept in order. Use draught excluder around the door and fit a jamb under it to fill in what is often a gaping hole. Make sure that the ventilators fit properly too.

Often a greenhouse has been erected on its foundation without any sealing. Consequently a strong draught enters around the base - you can easily check with a lighted match or candle in breezy weather. If this is the case, seal the gap with mastic squeezed from a tube, applying it when the surfaces are dry. Mastic can also be used to fill other small cracks found in the structure.

Having made the structure as draught-proof as possible the next step is to double glaze the interior. This can easily be done by lining it with clear polythene sheeting pinned or clipped to the glazing bars in order to trap a narrow layer of air between plastic and glass. Though more expensive to buy initially, I have found the bubble plastic now offered for the purpose to be far more effective. It is easier to put up since it does not stretch like polythene sheeting, and can be taken down when no longer required and stored for use again. What is more, this bubble plastic does not give the same condensation problems one experiences with ordinary polythene, which becomes loaded with droplets that shower down if the plastic is disturbed.

The nearer you can get to sealing your greenhouse completely, the less heat will be lost and wasted. If you use a gas or oil burner, however, do remember that it must have a supply of fresh air. Without enough oxygen such heaters fail to burn properly and become dangerous.

Where a greenhouse stands on a dwarf wall or has a boarded base, lining these with thick polystyrene sheeting will also help to conserve heat. So, too, will lining the lower part of a glass-to-ground greenhouse if your plants are all at bench level. If the greenhouse is fitted with external blinds, lowering these at night will further help reduce your fuel bills and keep up the temperature inside.

Partitioned Houses

It was the custom in large gardens for a propagation house to be divided into sections. That section at the end nearest the boiler was the hottest: that at the opposite end the coolest, possibly even unheated. Between would be one or two sections of varying warmth. Sowings could be started off in the warmest part and the seedlings moved progressively according to their needs and development through the different sections until they finally went out into a cold frame. The average garden greenhouse is too small to be built in this way, but something along the same lines can be usefully devised by erecting an internal partition, using battens to form a light framework that can be covered with bubble plastic. A single length of plastic that is weighted at the bottom but can be rolled up or moved when necessary can serve as a door. Alternatively, the house can be divided lengthwise to enclose one bench by attaching the plastic to the bars and allowing it to drape down along the front of the bench to ground level.

By partitioning your greenhouse in this way you can run one part at a much higher temperature from the rest without incurring too great a cost, or even heat only a portion of it. Where you intend to germinate plants that need a really brisk temperature to get them started, however, and especially any that demand an even temperature, an electric propagator is the answer.

Where seedlings need to be kept at a relatively high, even temperature for a while after germination, an electric thermostatically controlled propagator is convenient and economical to run. Do check that it is capable of giving a sufficiently high temperature lift (difference between outside and inside temperature) to meet your needs if the greenhouse is unheated.

An electric propagator is nothing more nor less than a self-contained, electrically heated frame. In size it can vary from being just large enough to take a single seed tray to a model that holds ten or more. The cover may be of plastic or glass and the heating should be thermostatically controlled for best results.

Small models can be used indoors on a wide windowsill if you do not have a greenhouse. But a larger size, that provides capacity for growing on seedlings for a while after they germinate, gives much more scope for a greenhouse owner. It is specially useful for early sowings in a moderately heated greenhouse. And provided the seeds are not put in too early, so that the seedlings will be safe on the greenhouse bench when they are removed from the propagator, it can be used to extend greatly the scope of an otherwise unheated greenhouse.

Automatic Ventilation Control

Seedlings grow best under glass when grown at a fairly even temperature, without being baked one minute and left shivering with cold the next. While the chief concern of anyone raising plants from seed in a greenhouse is maintaining an adequate minimum temperature, especially at night in winter and early spring, it is not long before it is necessary to keep down daytime temperatures as well. These can quickly exceed 90F (32C) when the sun shines. The chief method of doing this is by opening ventilators to allow the overheated air to escape and let cooler fresh air in. It requires a nicety of judgement and

Adjustable, self-contained, automatic vent controllers need no power supply and are easily fitted to most structures with screws or bolts. Once in operation they relieve you of the need for constant attendance to regulate greenhouse ventilation.

regular attendance to adjust the ventilation to meet the changing conditions through the day, something that most gardeners who go out to work are unable to provide. For this reason it is sensible to equip your greenhouse with some form of automatic ventilation control.

Provided electricity is available, the simplest and best method in a small greenhouse is to fit an extractor fan in the gable at one end, preferably the end facing north. This can be controlled by a thermostat so that it comes into operation at a pre-determined temperature to remove the hottest air which rises to the ridge of a greenhouse. But in order for a fan to operate effectively there must be a way for cool air to enter as well. In an ordinary structure there are plenty of places for this to occur, such as through the gaps where the panes of glass overlap and around the door. But if you have carefully draught-proofed and lined it with plastic to save heat you will need a partially open side ventilator as well, or an opening near ground level covered with a lightly-loaded spring shutter that can open inwards when the fan is pulling out the hot air.

Self-contained Units

Alternatively you can buy the self-contained units to open individual ventilators. These require no electricity and work by expansion as the temperature rises. I have used this type (mine are Bayliss Auto-Vents) for many years and found them to be most successful. They can be adjusted to meet your temperature requirements. But because they lag in operation a little behind the true temperature, it is best to adjust them to close at the right time, even if they are a little late in opening. Such automatic vent controllers are a boon to anyone who has to leave a greenhouse unattended during the day at any time of the year, as they can continuously adjust the air supply according to the internal temperature.

The only major drawback with this type of vent controller is that it cannot make allowance for strong wind that can knock plants about when the ventilators on the windward side are open. This problem does not arise, of course, when ventilation is controlled by an extractor fan.

Essential Thermometer

A maximum/minimum thermometer is an inexpensive yet essential piece of equipment for any greenhouse. In addition to showing the correct temperature, this type also records the highest and lowest temperatures that occur after setting it, which is best done every 24 hours. With its aid you can assess the efficiency not only of your heating system, but your ventilation technique as well. As with thermostats, it is best to place the thermometer at plant height since it is the degreee of warmth around the plants that matters; it should also be shielded from direct sunlight that could upset its readings. Adjustments to the setting of heaters and ventilators should be made according to the temperature recorded.

Watering Equipment

Watering plants under glass is another routine job that requires attention once a day, and at some seasons requires a considerable amount of time and effort. The best type of watering can to use is called a Haws' pattern (see page 92) and has a very long spout, making it easier to reach containers at the back of the staging. It should have both a coarse and a fine rose for watering plants at various stages of growth. Incidentally, when using the fine rose it should be fitted to the spout with the holes *upwards* so that the water is projected upwards and outwards to fall like fine rain.

For moistening plants and trays sown with seeds a pump-up hand sprayer is better still. The fine mist it produces will rewet soil that is beginning to dry out without panning the surface or disturbing the seeds. It is also the best type to use for watering really tiny seedlings - those of begonias and lobelias for instance - for a while after they are first patched out (see page 86). It takes a little longer, but avoids disturbing the plants because it cannot either wash them out or cover them with compost.

Capillary Watering Systems

To save the chore of watering individual containers there are a number of automatic watering systems available. One of the easiest and cheapest to instal is a capillary watering bench, which makes use of the existing staging. Simply cover the bench which can be the slatted type, with strong polythene sheeting and cover this in turn with capillary matting. It makes a more stable base for small pots if a sheet of hardboard is first laid over the slats, but this is not essential.

Capillary matting is a special material that absorbs water rather like blotting paper. If one edge of it is hung in a reservoir of water, the water moves through the material to saturate it. As the moisture evaporates or is taken up from the matting, more water moves into the material to take its place.

Moisture will also move by capillary action into pots and trays standing on the matting to keep the soil in them evenly moist, provided the compost is not too loose and makes firm contact with the matting. Plastic trays and pots, being thin, make good contact if pressed firmly in place and watered once by hand. There must, of course, be no crocks, shingle or other drainage material in the bottom of the containers to prevent the compost touching the matting. Clay pots, being much thicker, need to be provided with capillary wicks, such as Kerry Sticks, to bridge the space between the matting and the soil they contain. Apart from saving a great deal of work, capillary watering can result in sturdier seedlings and speedier growth, since the compost in which they are growing is kept evenly moist. When hand watering the moisture content of the soil fluctuates between fully wet to quite dry.

Making a Simple Reservoir

The water reservoir need not be elaborate. For example, a length of plastic guttering fitted with end closures and fixed along the edge of the bench works well, and I have used stout polythene sheeting securely pinned along the bench edge to form a kind of long narrow bag for the same purpose. Watering then becomes only a matter of topping up the reservoir once or twice a day, a job that is so simple anyone can do it for you without having to decide whether the plants need watering or not - a boon to anyone going on holiday.

To reduce attendance still further, the reservoir can be topped up from the mains via a small tank fitted with a float valve that will keep the water level at a predetermined height. If you do not have water laid on to the greenhouse you can still increase the reserve on the 'glug-bottle' principle. Most people will have noticed when washing up a milk-bottle, say, that a full bottle remains full as long as the opening is held under water. As soon as you lift it above water level air goes in and the water pours out. All you require therefore is a large airtight container that can be attached to the side of the greenhouse above bench level and fitted with a thin plastic tube. The open end of the tube is clipped inside the matting reservoir with the opening where the water level is to be maintained. When the water level drops below the end of the tube, water 'glugs' out of the large container until the tube opening is covered again.

Most home brew shops can offer a range of containers, bungs, tubing, as well as a tube clamp that can be used as a tap while a full container is being upended in place. Plastic containers are best, being light in weight and usually transparent enough for you to see the water level inside. Alternatively it is possible to buy a ready made kit for the purpose (see Appendix 7).

Other watering systems available can supply water direct to

individual pots or plants by means of flexible tubes and drip-nozzles, or mist units supplied from reservoirs or the mains. And if electricity as well as mains water is available, you can get very sophisticated equipment to control not only nozzle watering, but overhead watering, misting and damping down as well.

Electric Lighting

Where mains power is laid on to a greenhouse an electric light can be invaluable, especially early in the year when the days are short, allowing you to work there in the evenings. Although you can transport seedlings to a shed or kitchen when they need to be pricked out or potted off, it is much better not to risk them being chilled or blown about in a wind, by doing such jobs in the greenhouse all the time space is available.

As well as providing light for you to work by there are special lamps available for irradiating seedlings to augment the poor daylight early in the year, even to replace it in some cases. The light emitted by ordinary tungsten filament electric bulbs is too yellow for good plant growth, but these special lamps are designed to give a bluer light. Use of such artificial irradiation results in far sturdier seedlings and, most important, quicker development. Irradiated tomato seedlings sown in January or February, for instance, can begin cropping weeks earlier if given sufficient light during the first six weeks of growth. Such lamps are specially useful to anyone who raises plants from seed indoors in late winter or spring in particular, where natural light is much weaker even than in a greenhouse.

Useful Accessories

For working in a greenhouse a portable potting bench, that can be stood on the staging or span the path between two benches, is very useful. It is the sort of thing that handy people can quickly knock-up for themselves from wood or plywood. A simple potting bench consists of a base of suitable size, but preferably not less than 2 ft (60 cm) wide by 1½ ft (45 cm) deep, with a 12 in (30 cm) high back, and sides that taper down to a narrow lip at the front. Compost is piled at the rear of the bench, leaving the front clear for filling pots and trays when sowing seeds or pricking out and potting on young plants. There is also at least one purpose-made aluminium portable potting bench on the market which, at the time of writing, is priced under £10.

Useful items you can make for yourself are pressers of various sizes to fit the pots and trays you commonly use. These can be cut from ¼ in (5 mm) plywood and a wooden handle pinned and glued to the top.

Given a coat of polyurethane varnish they will last for years and are invaluable for creating a firm level surface that is essential when seed sowing. It is also worth buying a Dibalot. This is a presser moulded in plastic with projections on the base. It fits a standard half-tray and compresses the compost and marks the positions for plants in one go when pricking out.

Tapering dibbers of various sizes can be whittled from wood or dowelling to make the holes when pricking out plants and sowing large seeds. One of about pencil thickness is the most useful. Indeed I frequently use a pencil for the purpose. Keep them together with a blunt table knife or thin plastic spatula which can be used to lift groups of tiny seedlings from their trays or pots, when pricking out, without a great deal of root damage.

Clear labelling is essential at all stages if plants are not to become muddled. My own preference is for Hartley aluminium labels. Although expensive to buy initially they can be written on with ordinary lead pencil on both sides and are easily wiped clean again using a little scouring powder on a damp cloth. Consequently they are good for several seasons. They also remain legible for a number of years out of doors, where they cannot rot and, thanks to their metallic colouring, are easily found. They are specially useful, therefore, when raising perennial plants since the same labels can remain with them throughout their lives.

Keeping the greenhouse glass spotlessly clean is essential when raising plants early in the year in order for them to benefit as much as possible from natural daylight. A barely discernible layer of grime can reduce the light intensity by 10% which - when light is the limiting factor to plant growth - must reduce their development. Ideally the glass should be cleaned at least fortnightly at that time. One of those car-washing brushes that can be attached to a hosepipe so that you have a trickle of water running through the bristles as you use it speeds up the job. Alternatively, tie the end of your hosepipe to the handle of a soft broom to serve the same purpose. The longer handle makes it easier to reach the ridge of the roof without needing a stepladder.

Early Sowings in Your Home

It can be surprising to anyone who has never tried it just how many plants can be raised from seed in the home, without using special equipment of any kind, apart from a few pots and trays of compost and plastic bags. In a home environment you can usually find all that is necessary to provide protection and warmth for germinating exotic as well as hardy plants. The only drawback is usually a lack of light intensity and, as we have seen, without sufficient light seedlings tend to become drawn and lanky. It may also be less convenient for you, too.

Nevertheless many people do raise a great many plants indoors, tackling those that would otherwise be denied them, and very successfully. I would not suggest that the seedlings are always as good as those raised under ideal greenhouse conditions, but they give a great deal of satisfaction to their raisers. And, despite all the drawbacks, a keen gardener can often have as good, if not better plants, than someone with every conceivable aid who fails to give his plants proper attention. So let's have a look at the possibilities.

Using Airing Cupboard Warmth

First and foremost aid to early indoor sowings is an airing cupboard which can make an ideal germinating chamber for all seeds that appreciate warmth, yet do not need light at this stage. Indeed, I often use it to start off seedlings of plants that are to be grown on in a cold greenhouse. Such crops as Brussels sprouts, cabbage and lettuce for really early pickings can be started this way. So, too, can those hardy perennial border plants, like delphiniums and lupins, which will flower well in their first summer if started off early. Half-hardy annual bedding plants, such as French marigolds and nemesia, also respond

An airing cupboard serves as an excellent 'propagator' for germinating seeds of a variety of plants. Do look at them morning and evening, however, and remove any tray or pot to a light place at the first sign of the shoots pushing through the soil.

well to such treatment, as do those tender marrows and cucumbers, provided that sowings are timed to ensure that there is no chance of them being frosted when moved to an unheated greenhouse or frame. There is no doubt in my mind that quick germination gets seedlings off to the best start. Even tender plants that need quite a brisk heat in order to germinate often grow well, if slowly, in a comparatively low temperature if you can once get them up.

The snag with an airing cupboard, of course, is that it is dark. Once the seedlings push through the covering of compost they must be moved into a well-lit position. Provided care is taken to cover the seeds evenly with compost, the seedlings of most ordinary plants usually come up more or less together. You can ignore the first one or two to appear, and if they become excessively lanky they can be thrown away later. Instead, wait until a reasonable number appear before removing the container from the airing cupboard. I find it is essential to examine such sowings night and morning to be sure of catching them at the right stage. Development of some kinds is so swift they can be spoiled in 24 hours.

Use Plastic Bags

Provided you take my tip to put newly-sown containers in clean, clear polythene bags there will be no mess and no need for watering, which will go far to maintain domestic harmony! It is as well to check the temperature of the airing cupboard beforehand, preferably with a maximum/minimum thermometer, that can be used to record the highest and lowest temperatures reached during a 24-hour period. These can vary according to the water temperature maintained, the efficiency of the lagging jacket on the tank and how well the door fits. The overnight temperature can drop if the water heater is switched off at night - dramatically so in winter if the hot water in the tank is drained out for late night baths. It is also sensible to check the temperature at different heights inside the cupboard, since it can vary considerably between floor and ceiling.

For some tender plants, like F1 hybrid geraniums and impatiens, a steady temperature is essential for good germination. And, while most tender plants develop well at a temperature of about 70F (21C), most hardy plants and vegetables will do better in the range of 60-65F (16-18C). It is helpful, therefore, to know which part of an airing cupboard is likely best to suit the seeds you have sown.

A dark airing cupboard will not do for those seeds that need light in order to germinate. Nor is it necessarily a good place for those that need a constant, even heat should the temperature fluctuate appreciably. An airing cupboard can actually be too hot in some cases, especially near the top, if the hot-water cylinder is not well lagged.

The best place indoors for growing seeds that germinate only in light is an electrically-heated propagator placed on a windowsill. Although it tends to provide less even warmth, for unheated containers a spot near an oil-fired boiler, or even a tray standing on top of it, can be utilised to start germination. But beware of solid fuel boilers that often emit fumes when being stoked. Such fumes can quickly damage tender seedlings.

Once the seedlings appear the plastic coverings must be removed from the containers, which should then be placed in a well-lit situation. Those of tender plants must also receive enough warmth.

Kitchen and Bathroom

The best room in a house for growing plants is often the kitchen. Where it is in constant use this is often the warmest and most humid room in the house. Bathrooms, too, if heated and not too small can be useful, again because the air in them tends to be more humid. What is more upstairs rooms are often brighter because less of the sky light is blocked by other buildings and trees. Humidity is essential because too dry an atmosphere can retard leaf development and, consequently, growth as well. The drier the air the quicker moisture is lost through leaves. Plants therefore have to balance leaf growth with the amount of moisture they can absorb through their roots.

It is no use having too much warmth and humidity if light is lacking because this is often the factor that limits plant growth, early in the year especially. Without sufficient light intensity to provide energy to enable them to manufacture food in their leaves, plants quickly become pale and spindly. So where light intensity tends to be low, it is better to keep seedlings on the cool side, though their tolerance varies and most tender plants will be decidedly unhappy in a temperature that is less than 60F (16C) for most of the time. On the other hand very high temperatures will increase their tendency to become pale and leggy.

Obviously, therefore, it pays to pick the brightest windowsill you can find for raising seedlings indoors. A bay window that allows in daylight on three sides is better than an ordinary window. And the light can be further improved if a reflector is mounted on the fourth side to throw at least some light on to the plants from that direction. A piece of hardboard painted white or covered with shiny kitchen foil works well, especially if it extends to 10 in (25 cm) higher than the plants so that their tops receive plenty of reflected light. Even a length of white sheet hung as a curtain can be surprisingly effective.

To further increase the amount of reflected light it helps if the container holding pots or trays is also painted white. So, too, can surfacing the compost the seeds are growing in with a thin layer of Perlite. This light- weight material will remain at the surface after each watering to maintain a near-white layer. Special electric lights can be used to supplement or even replace daylight where necessary.

Beware of Draughts

One trouble to beware of when raising plants indoors is draughts. Plants can be just as uncomfortable as you can in a chilling draught and, unfortunately, windows do tend to be draughty. It is as well therefore to do your best to draught-proof any window where you intend to raise plants indoors. This is easily accomplished with self-adhesive tape. But apart from preventing cold air entering around windows that open, there is the problem of air which is cooled on contact with the glass and flows down like an unseen waterfall. If you arrange boards across a bay window to form a bench or stand a table in the window, leave a 2 in (5 cm) space along the front edge for this cool air to pass through. If you do not it will flow across the plants and chill them. Windows can be particularly cold spots at night and plants should never be trapped between the curtains and the glass in winter and spring. It is best if they can be moved into the room before you draw the curtains.

To help maintain a good level of humidity about the seedlings the pots or boxes in which they are growing are best stood on trays of aggregate that can be kept moist. Sand and gravel are often used, but light-weight Perlite makes it easier to move the trays when necessary, and is usually a better light reflector. A table can be equipped with a temporary top for the purpose. All you need to do is make a surround of wood to act as a tray edge to stand on the table, line it with a double thickness of heavy-duty polythene sheeting (after making sure there are not holes in it!) and fill it almost to the brim with peat or Perlite. If you cover the table with a thick layer of newspaper first, to prevent any possibility of scratching, it will come to no harm. I have used such a tray in the window of a centrally-heated room with great success and there is no doubt that the seedlings appreciated the extra humidity.

Plant Raising in Garden Rooms

The best place of all for raising seedlings in the home, perhaps, is a purpose-built garden room, which, having plenty of window area, is very well lit. Here the controlling factor will probably be the night temperature. If it drops too low it will be unsuitable for the more tender plants early in the year and you may have to adjust the normal sowing time to allow for this. A glazed porch, especially a south facing one, can also offer a great many possibilities for raising seedlings. But again, beware of sowing tender plants too early.

Apart from seedlings that will eventually be planted outdoors, or perhaps moved to an unheated greenhouse or frame, a great many can be grown to maturity in pots indoors. These not only include those recognised as house plants, like *Hypoestes sanguinolenta*, the polka-dot plant, colourful-leaved coleus, dainty asparagus ferns and finger-leaved *Aralia sieboldii*, but many half-hardy annuals and greenhouse flowers, too, that make charming and unusual pot plants given a sufficiently well-lit spot.

But you are not restricted to ornamental plants alone. A wide range of herbs can be easily raised from seed and grown on in pots in a sunny window or transplanted to a window box. Minibel is a very small bush tomato that can be grown to perfection in a 5 in (12.5 cm) pot on a windowsill; its fruits are small but nonetheless welcome. Fembaby and Petita are two cucumbers that can be grown in pots on a window and trained up canes. Their fruits are shorter than greenhouse varieties, being 6-7 in (15-18 cm) long, but just as delicious.

Mustard and Cress

Mustard and cress, which is nothing more than the seedling shoots of these two plants gathered when a few days old, is an easy salad crop to produce indoors at any time of year. The traditional method is to scatter the cress seeds thinly over a tray of firmed compost, then just press the seeds into the surface. Keep the tray moist in a warm dark place for three days, then sow the quicker-growing mustard and return the tray to its dark position. When the pale yellow shoots have been drawn up to about 1½ in (4 cm) high, bring the tray into a well-lit place so the leaves will turn green. Then cut as required. Even simpler and quicker to produce is salad rape, which is sown and grown in exactly the same way, except that you use only one lot of seed. This, incidentally, is what is usually sold instead of mustard and cress in shops these days.

Since these salads can be produced solely from the food stored in the seeds there is no need to use any soil at all and I usually grow them on a moist paper kitchen towel. Use a clean 5 in (12.5 cm) plastic half-pot. Fold a piece of kitchen towel into four and cut it to fit into the base of the pot. Use a piece cut off to act as a wick, pushing it partly through one of the drainage holes before covering the base with the shaped paper. Stand the pot on three or four washed pebbles in a dish so that it is supported ½ in (1 cm) above the base.

Pour enough water into the pot to saturate the paper, then more into the dish until it almost touches the pot base. Scatter the seeds thinly over the paper and leave them to shoot.

Stand the dish on the kitchen windowsill and cover the pot with a piece of cardboard to keep it dark at first then expose the seedlings to the light when large enough. When ready the mustard and cress are easily removed, complete with paper to make it easy to cut the shoots with scissors. By sowing two or three pots at intervals and resowing when each batch is harvested, a regular supply of this salad is easily maintained for a few minutes work every 2-3 days without mess or fuss.

Sprouting Seeds

Sprouting seeds have become very popular in recent years as salads and vegetables. Best known is Mung beans (Chinese bean sprouts), but Adzuki beans, fenugreek, alfalfa and radish can also be grown in this way to provide unusual tasty food. They are very quick and easy to produce, needing neither soil nor sun and the only equipment required is a clean glass jar, a piece of muslin to cover the top and an elastic band to hold it in place. Put a small quantity of seed into the jar (remember they will swell when wetted and take up even more space as the shoots form), cover the top with muslin, then half-fill it with luke-warm water. Swirl the water around to wash the seeds thoroughly then pour it off through the muslin and repeat the process.

From then on wash the seeds through once in the same way each morning and evening until ready to eat, which usually takes 3-6 days. The best place to keep the jar - which should be laid on its side - is in a warm cupboard, but any warm, preferably dark place will do. And should you wish to sprout them in really large quantities, perhaps for a special party, obtain a plastic sweet bottle which, being flat-sided, will not roll about.

Like any other vegetable sprouted seeds are best eaten as soon as they are ready, but will keep well in closed plastic bags in a refrigerator for a week. The only disadvantage I have found with them is that some batches need to be carefully checked through for any seeds which do not sprout, as they can be very hard on the teeth and off-putting to say the least. But sprouted seeds can be very welcome, especially in winter - when fresh food from the garden is usually in such short supply.

7. Making a Lawn from Seed

One of the first major gardening jobs undertaken by most people, faced with a brand new empty plot, is to create a lawn. Many, in the interests of speed, choose to make their new lawn from turf. Yet producing a new lawn from seed is not all that slow and can be achieved at a fraction of the cost. What is more, by raising your own lawn from seed you can choose a mixture best suited to your particular site and purpose, and you will not import weeds or any other problems. In any case the work of preparing the site is largely the same whether it is to be turfed or sown.

The times for sowing grass seed are April and early September; the latter is, perhaps, the better since you are likely to have less need to water the sown area. On the other hand an April sowing allows for a full season of development before the onset of winter. Certainly by that time the new 'sward' should be fully established and well-knit, though it will look presentable long before then.

The technique of sowing a lawn - where you want to establish a permanent close-knit community of plants - is different from that for any other type of plant. But the same conditions are as necessary for good germination of grass as they are for other seeds and a good surface seedbed must be prepared. But beneath the surface, the initial preparation must be even more thorough. Any lack of consolidation will result in subsidence later, which is the cause for those annoying humps and hollows that mar so many garden lawns. You must also bring the surface as near flat as possible.

Ground Preparation

Your plans for preparation must take account of the fact that a lawn will be a permanent feature of the garden - for many years to come. Any scrimping or shortcomings in preparing the ground will be difficult to deal with once the grass is established. Grass roots are mainly confined to the top 6 in (15 cm) of soil and this needs to be well drained and aerated, yet continual foot traffic and passage of a mower tends to pack it down too hard, especially if the soil is clay.

Moss and weed problems usually associated with garden lawns are largely due to the failure to prepare the ground properly first. When over-compaction eventually occurs grass growth falters and weeds and moss then colonise the spaces. And once in they are difficult to rout out again. It can save enormous effort and expense later if you do your best to improve the soil beforehand.

Ideally preparation should be started some months ahead of sowing, which allows time not only for the soil to settle, but also for weed seeds in the surface to germinate and be killed off to give the grass seedlings a really clean start. If large amounts of soil have to be moved to level the site the work is best done in the autumn so that it has the benefit of winter rain to reconsolidate it. Where the levels are only an inch or two (2-5 cm) out, levelling is a comparatively simple business. Where more than this is needed the top soil should be stripped from half the site in turn, the sub-soil levelled and the top soil spread evenly on top again. If not you could end up with only a few inches of fertile top soil left in some places, which is not enough to support the healthy growth of grass. A lawn does not have to be strictly level, unless you specially want a good playing surface for games, but the surface should preferably be *flat* like a table top - even if it tilts in one direction or another.

Soil Improvement

Having adjusted the soil levels where necessary the next step is to try to improve the texture of heavy soil to ensure it will be sufficiently well aerated. This is done by working coarse, sharp sand into the top 6 in (15 cm). And in order to bring about a satisfactory improvement it may take as much as a 6-in (15-cm) layer of sand, spread over the soil and thoroughly worked in with a mechanical cultivator. This will, of course, raise the final soil level significantly, which should be allowed for. But the lasting improvement of the sward where this is done really does make the effort and expense worthwhile on clay ground.

The reason that large quantities of sand are needed is due to the properties of clay, which are far more powerful and therefore dominant in any soil (see page 22). What seems to be a really heavy, sticky area probably contains no more than 15-20% of clay. In order to reduce that percentage by half, the bulk must be doubled - that is 6 in (15 cm) of sand mixed with 6 in (15 cm) of soil.

Where the soil is very light and sandy the problem is not one of lack of drainage and aeration, but excessive aeration and dryness in spring and summer. Here an addition of clay to the soil could bring about improvement but is by no means so easily done, even if you could obtain a supply. Instead, the best answer is to work organic matter - preferably in the form of weed-free moss peat or composted bark - into the soil to increase its humus content and moisture-holding ability.

Final preparation for sowing should be carried out in March, as soon as the soil dries out if the ground was dug and levelled the previous autumn. But if the work is done in summer for September sowing and little levelling was needed, the process can follow on immediately.

Begin by applying a dressing of general fertiliser, such as Growmore, at 2 oz per sq yd (50 g per sq m) and work this into the soil. Then tread the whole area thoroughly and rake the surface, repeating the process until your heels no longer sink into the soil. The repeated treading and raking will break down any lumps. Any stones, twigs or other rubbish should be raked up and removed each time. You

Time spent in the creation of a fine surface tilth pays dividends by helping you to get speedy germination.

should now have a completely firm, flat, well-consolidated area that is rubbish-free on top. The actual area should be 6 in (15 cm) wider all round than the lawn required. Then, when the grass is established, you can cut back to the required line to make a neat, firm edge.

Finishing the Surface

To bring the surface soil to the highest finish, drag a heavy board held on its edge across the complete site. This will pare soil from any high spots which can be raked into the low areas untouched by the board and trodden firm. The longer the board the more even the result will be, but you will need an assistant to help you drag a really long board. An alternative way, if you have to work single-handed, is to attach a length of line to a heavy, unwarped (many are not) ladder. Dragging this flat across the area has the same effect as the board, planing soil off the high spots and revealing the low ones, by leaving them untouched. Once you are satisfied the area is as flat as you can get it, go over it again with a rake just to loosen the surface and erase any marks. But take special pains not to move the soil into fresh ridges.

If at all possible try to reach this stage 3-6 weeks ahead of sowing. Then there will be time for the first flush, and preferably two, of weed seedlings to germinate. These should be killed off by hoeing or the use of a paraquat/diquat weedkiller. Using a weedkiller has a great advantage in that it does not disturb the soil in any way. When you come to sow the grass seed, first rake the area very lightly, just deep enough for the teeth of the rake to make shallow furrows.

The seed mixture to sow will depend on the use to which you intend to put the area of grass. If the new lawn is to be mainly for show a superfine mixture can be used. If it is likely that children and animals will play on it a mixture of tougher species will be better. The usual lawn grasses do not grow well in shade under trees, but most seed firms offer special mixtures for shady areas. Even these will not flourish in deep shade, however, and if this is likely to be a future problem such areas are better paved or filled with ground-cover plants.

Cheap mixtures of hard-wearing grass seeds frequently contain perennial ryegrass which, though suitable for a playing field is really too coarse for a good-looking garden lawn. It tends to swamp the finer grasses that in any case should be trimmed shorter. Better class utility mixtures used to contain no ryegrass at all, but in recent years dwarf forms of perennial ryegrass have become available that make a perfectly satisfactory sward. When choosing a mixture containing ryegrass, therefore, do make sure that it is a dwarf form that is included and not the ordinary perennial ryegrass.

Sowing Rates

Grass seed is sown quite thickly, but can be overdone. Overcrowding is just as bad for grass seedlings as any other kind. The sowing rate is assessed in ounces per square yard (grams per square metre) and varies from 1-1½ oz (25-40 g) according to the species used. The finer grasses generally have smaller seeds and so you need less weight of these to produce the same number of plants. Although superfine

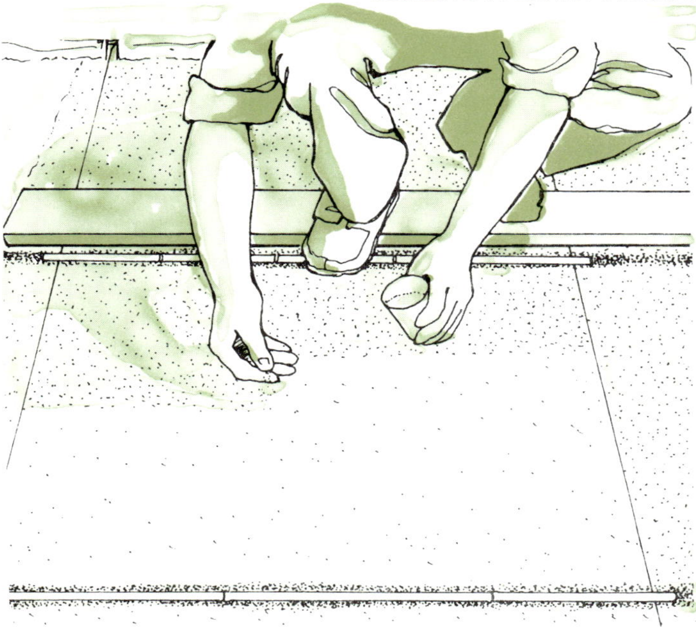

Where the area is not too big, divide it into square yards (square metres) as you go using two lines crossed with canes and sow each in turn.

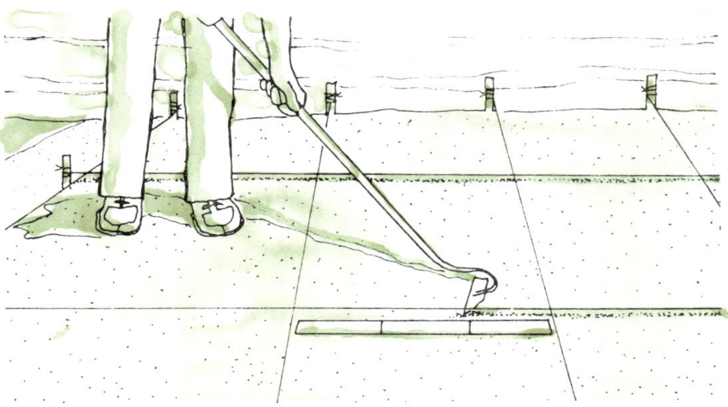

Alternatively, use a line and hoe to mark out the whole area into square yards (square metres) before you begin sowing the seeds.

mixtures cost much more per pound, when you calculate the total quantity of seed needed they can prove to be little more expensive to sow than the larger-seeded coarser grasses. It is worth paying a little extra to have the seed treated with a bird repellent. If not birds can take a surprising quantity of seed and leave you with thin patches that may need to be resown, which is annoying to say the least.

Every care must be taken to sow grass seed evenly so that you get an even stand of grass that will quickly expand to make a well-knit expanse of turf. Over a small area this can be done by sowing in blocks measuring 1 square yard (1 square metre). Put down two lines 1 yd (1 m) apart and place two canes across them at one end to mark off 1 square yard (1 square metre). Scatter the required amount of seed evenly over this area, then move the first cane 1 yd (1 m) beyond the second to mark the next square yard (square metre) and so on. It is a very efficient method and is not as slow as it sounds, provided you make a measure for the seeds. To do this you need only weigh out the amount needed for one square yard (1 square metre), put it into a narrow glass or clear plastic container, give it a shake to settle the seeds, then mark their height on the container with a piece of sticky tape. From then on simply fill the container to the mark each time, dispensing the measure of grass seed as evenly as possible over the allotted square.

Alternative Methods

Where the area to be grassed is too great to use this method you have two alternatives. One is to use a wheeled distributor that drops the seeds evenly in a wide band as you push it over the site. Some of the garden lawn fertiliser distributors can be adjusted for this purpose. When using such a distributor work up and down the plot taking special care to see that each band neatly joins the one before without overlapping.

The other method is to broadcast the seed by hand, like the sowers of old. Choose a still day for the job and first divide the seed into four equal amounts. Scatter each of these as evenly as you can while working in a different direction over the site - up, down and across - which increases your chances of getting an even coverage. It is not easy to scatter seed in this way unless you are used to it and the best technique, I find, is to hold a good pinch between fingers and thumb and release it gradually while flicking the wrist from side to side so that the seeds spray out in a broad arc each time. Even then, it is a method I would use only as a last resort.

Once the seeds are sown the final job is to press them down in contact with the soil with a light roller. The one at the rear of most cylinder lawnmowers will do if you draw the machine backwards while holding the front roller off the ground to keep the blades well clear of the soil. Or you can simply pat the soil down firmly with the back of a spade or shovel. Provided you gently raked the ground before sowing the rake teeth will have made very shallow furrows. Any seed that fell in them will be just buried or partially covered during the rolling, while the rest on top of the soil will now be pressed into the surface.

Keep It Moist

From this time until the grass seed germinates make sure the soil does not dry out. The seeds are not covered completely like most others and are more likely to suffer from lack of rain and drying winds as a consequence. This is one of the reasons that April and September are the best sowing times for a garden lawn. It is quite usual then to have heavy dews and the soil is often moist on the surface in the mornings. It is not necessary to keep the soil wet all the time, but it is a wise precaution to keep a hosepipe and sprinkler handy. Keeping the soil moist also discourages birds and cats from digging in it. If the seeds sown were not treated with a bird repellent you should string black cotton quite thickly over the area to stop birds making a meal of them. Should you be unable to water the site after preparation, then keep an eye on the weather forecasts and try to sow when an unsettled, showery period is expected.

The first sign of germination is the appearance of what seems to be a green haze over the area and this can be seen much more clearly if you get down on your knees and look across the site close to the ground. It is then not long before you can distinguish the developing shoots with ease. Continue to water if necessary to prevent the soil from drying out.

Once the young grass shoots are about 2 in (5 cm) high, lightly roll the area again to refirm the surface which will have been loosened as the shoots pushed through. This rolling will also encourage the young plants to 'tiller', or make fresh shoots from the base. Don't worry about the plants being pushed flat; they will soon stand up again. A few days later the new grass will need to be 'topped' by removing about ½ in (1 cm) of its growth. This is best done with shears or a hand cylinder mower from which the front roller has been removed to stop it pressing down the grass ahead of the blades. Whichever you use, the blades must be really sharp and cut well, otherwise many of the tiny plants may be dragged out by the roots.

Mow Regularly

Following this tipping a regular routine of weekly mowing should be begun, gradually reducing the height of cut each time until you reach that recommended for the type of grass you have sown - ½-¾ in (1-1.5 cm) for superfine grass mixtures, or 1-1¼ in (2-2.5 cm) for utility lawns - the shorter figure being the summer height to aim for.

Provided the ground was prepared in good time for weed seedlings to germinate and be killed before the grass seed was sown, weeds should not prove to be a serious problem in the new lawn. Careful hand weeding can be done if there are still a lot of weeds in the early stages, but there is always the danger of pulling up grass seedlings with them. Once mowing begins, however, all but lawn weeds quickly disappear since they cannot stand such treatment. Alternatively the selective lawn weedkiller called Actrilawn, which is specially formulated for use on young grass, can be used to deal with these. Ordinary lawn weedkillers are too strong to be safely used on grass seedlings less than one year old. Nor should any supplementary feeding be needed if the ground was correctly prepared.

It is only a matter of weeks from sowing time before your new area of grass will actually look like a lawn, but do not be misled by its appearance. The grass seedlings will take at least six months to become well established and should not be given rough usage during this period.

8. Growing Plants from Pips and Stones

Once hooked on raising one's own plants from seed and having found out just how easy it can be, an enterprising person soon tries their hand at growing plants from odd fruit pips and stones and other seeds that may come their way. Although some of these may take a year or more to do anything, others can be quick. In the case of exotic fruits you are not likely to grow a plant to fruiting size, unless you have a huge greenhouse and can afford to heat it the year round. But many such seedlings make excellent house plants, and certainly add a touch of novelty to the display as well as being a talking point with fellow enthusiasts.

I have mentioned elsewhere the difficulty of raising a really first class apple from a pip, but there are still some nameless trees to be found in old gardens bearing acceptable fruit that were produced this way. Indeed, that was how most of the old varieties which are still grown were produced, if not found growing wild in some hedgerow or wood; even those apples introduced in the past by nurserymen. It is only in comparatively modern times that planned breeding was carried out, first by nursery firms, then by independently sponsored and government research stations. Our best known dessert apple is Cox's Orange Pippin, while Bramley's Seedling still leads the field as a cooker. The former was raised in 1825 by Mr Cox, who was a retired brewer of Colnbrook Lawn. Mr Bramley was a shoemaker in Southwell, Nottinghamshire. What would the best apples be today, I wonder, if they had not bothered to sow some pips? So although there is always a large element of chance, the wheel of fortune does sometimes click to the winning number.

This element of chance applies when raising new seedlings of all the fruits normally grown out of doors in this country, though the odds do vary. The chances of raising a good gooseberry, for instance, are quite high. Over a hundred different varieties were recorded by E.A.Bunyard in *A Handbook of Hardy Fruits* published in 1925. Most of these were raised between 1825 and 1875 when, in the days before fruit was plentifully imported, gooseberries were in their hey-day.

Strangely it is not an indigenous fruit at all but the peach which gives you the best chance of raising a really first class fruiting tree. So many examples are to be found of people who have enjoyed eating peaches from a tree they raised from a stone and planted in the garden that it seems one can hardly miss.

Most pips and stones of hardy fruits need to be either stratified or sown in autumn and exposed to frost and snow to get good germination. I have, however, found apple pips shooting in a rotted apple under a tree in late summer, so possibly seeds sown before they are fully ripe may germinate quickly in some cases. Once germinated, growth is often quite swift and an apple seedling can easily make 12-18 in (30-45 cm) of growth in its first year. And while it is easy and safer to grow them in pots at first, to avoid them being overlooked and possibly damaged when small, they do not need to be coddled. In fact the best place for them is a well-ventilated cold frame until they are large enough to be safely set out of doors.

Citrus Fruits are Simple

Among the exotic types, lemons and other citrus fruits are easy and rewarding. Simply remove a few pips the next time you are cutting up a fruit. Leave them for a day or two on the kitchen windowsill to dry off, then sow them ¼ in (5 mm) deep in a small pot of suitable compost. Water the pot thoroughly and, after leaving it a while to drain, put it into a plastic bag to keep it moist. You can either leave the pot on the windowsill, or speed germination by putting it in a warm airing cupboard or propagator where the seedlings usually appear in 2-6 weeks.

Once up the seedlings can be set individually in small pots and grown on. Citrus plants are evergreen and should never be allowed to become dry at the root, and it is best if they are protected from frost. Although they do not mind warmth they can stand cool conditions well enough. In fact we had one grapefruit that survived many winters in an unheated room.

Thanks to their ornamental foliage, date palms look quite showy and can be raised from the stones found in those boxes of fruit sold at Christmas time. They seem to be rather erratic in the time they take to germinate and are certainly better for keeping warm. The easiest way I have found is merely to push them into the soil of another pot plant where they will germinate as often as not without special treatment. Once up however, the seedlings should be carefully moved into small pots of their own. But if you want to be more professional about it, sow them in a pot of sowing compost and keep it in a warm place, covering it with polythene to keep it moist.

The true date palm is *Phoenix dactylifera*, which develops into quite

Oranges, lemons and grapefruit plants are easy to raise and make interesting pot plants. Wash and dry the pips before sowing. Top: Cover them with about ½ inch (1 cm) of soil in a pot. If you use a peat compost simply push them down into it and level the surface. Below: Kept in a warm place the seeds germinate readily, appearing in 2-6 weeks.

a large plant that can soon outgrow its welcome! The two species normally grown as house plants are *P. canariensis* and *P. robelinii*, seeds of which are usually available from one or other of the seed firms.

Avocado pears contain a huge seed about the size and shape of an egg. House plant enthusiasts often germinate these to obtain an unusual plant. When my wife and I were running a fresh-food restaurant some years ago it was not unusual for patrons to leave clutching a stone or two wrapped in a paper napkin for the purpose. Avocado stones are best sown in a pot of moist compost and germinated at a high temperature of about 80F (27C). But a novel way is to stand the stone on a water-filled jar having a neck just narrow enough to prevent the stone falling in, so that the base of the stone touches the water. When it germinates the stone splits apart to allow the shoot to grow. Once it reaches this stage do not delay too long before planting it in a pot.

If you buy your coffee from a supplier who actually roasts the beans in his shop - and what a delicious aroma that creates! - see if he can provide you with a few plump, fresh, unroasted ones. These are the seeds of *Coffea*, which can develop into handsome house plants with glossy, deep green leaves. The beans must be fresh, however, since they soon lose their powers of germination. And if you do not have a local coffee shop, you can obtain them from several of the major seed firms.

Coffee beans need a lot of warmth to germinate swiftly and the sown containers should be started off in a temperature of about 80F (27C), which means using a propagator or airing cupboard. Once up they can be grown on at ordinary room temperature. The plants are evergreen, hate draughts and should never be allowed to dry out. Although they can survive winter at a minimum temperature of 50F (10C), they seem much happier in warmer conditions. When suitable a coffee plant can develop into a large bush, but you can restrict its size by pruning it in spring.

Plants can be raised from fresh cobnuts and chestnuts sown in pots in an outdoor frame. Indeed, the cobnut is a useful plant if you want to try your hand at growing a miniature Bonzai tree. These must be fresh, however - all too often cobnuts have poor wizened kernels due to being stored for too long.

Although hardly decorative, a peanut is a fascinating plant and one that will flower and fruit. Those fresh, shelled nuts which some shops

---

Facing page: Pot the young citrus plants into individual small pots as soon as the seed leaves have expanded. At this stage there is only a single short fleshy root (above) and they receive little check to growth. Plant them at roughly the same depth as before (below) or a little deeper if the stem has become drawn due to lack of light or competition.

sell often germinate, and you should have little difficulty if you are lucky enough to get some still in their shells. Sow the nuts in pots in spring, keep them warm and they soon germinate. Later plant the

The seed or 'nut' of an avocado can be sown in a pot of compost, but gives added fascination if germinated by the water method, since you can see what is going on. Balance the seed so that its rounded base just touches the water in a bottle or jar. If the neck is too wide to support the seed, thrust a wooden cocktail stick into either side of it as shown here. Once the root system is well formed (the seedling will live on the food stored in the seed at first) pot it up leaving the nose of the nut just showing above the surface.

seedlings in a trough or large pot and train their rather sprawling stems across the soil. In late summer pale orange pea-like flowers appear. Later the flower stalks bend over and grow longer, forcing the ovaries at their tips into the soil where the pods develop and ripen. In effect, it is a plant that sows its own seeds about it, and it is no wonder they are also called ground-nuts.

If you have a packet of bird seed and feel the urge to experiment, why not try sowing some? Provided it is not so old as to have lost all viability you could get a strange selection of plants and grasses, some of which are ornamental. Indeed, the odd plants that sometimes appear in the soil close to where a bird cage is regularly hung often puzzle people. Try treating any seedlings that germinate as you would half-hardy annuals, planting them out of doors towards the end of May or early June when the danger of a late frost in your area is passed.

You can try your luck too, with the seeds in dried chillies and other fresh spices which, if they come up, can add a touch of adventure to your gardening. Generally, these will have to be grown in a greenhouse or indoors since they mostly need warmth. The chief thing with such 'adventure sowing' is to have a go. You never know what the results will be, and it costs no more than a little time and a handful or two of compost to try!

9. Raising Ferns from Spores

Although they are commonly listed in seed catalogues, ferns are out of the run of usual plants you are likely to raise for the reason that they neither flower nor produce seeds. What is actually sold in the packets are spores. These are more dust-like than any seeds and need rather special conditions in order to grow. But anyone prepared to take the trouble can easily satisfy their needs and enjoy what is one of the most intriguing ways of raising plants.

It was not until the invention of the microscope opened up a previously unseen world that the way in which ferns reproduced

As well as scalding the pot, soak the compost with boiling water to sterilise it completely.

themselves was revealed. And how strange it proved to be, because ferns have no sexual organs on the mature plants. Instead they produce millions of these dusty minute spores from the *sori*, those round brown patches or lines usually found on the reverse sides of their leaves.

Under suitably moist conditions the spores germinate and produce a *prothalus*, a green plate-like structure, on the underside of which the *antheridia* (male) and *archegonia* (female) reproductive organs develop. When mature the antheridia release spermatozoids which swim free through water to reach and fertilise the archegonia. Only then can young fern plants develop on the prothali, which soon wither once the young plants have their own leaves and roots.

As you can see, there are two distinct stages of development. And in order for these to be successfully completed, the surface on which the spores lie must be kept permanently moist and fairly shaded for some weeks while both stages take place. In addition you must try and rule out any possibility of an invasion of mosses, algae and fungi, which also use spores in order to reproduce themselves. Various methods have been suggested over the years for raising ferns from spores, but here is the one I have used with complete success.

You will need a 6 in (15 cm) plastic pot, a pot saucer in which to stand it, and a clear plastic dome to fit over the top. I use peat potting compost as the sowing medium, but a soil-based one should be equally successful.

Preparations for Sowing

The first stage is to get the pot and cover as clean as possible by giving them a thorough wash. Then, to make sure there is no possibility of carrying unwanted spores on them, scald them with boiling water. Now fill the pot with the potting compost, pressing it down quite firmly to produce a level surface. Having done this, water it with boiling water, giving enough to soak the whole pot. This will sterilise the compost surface and kill off any spores that are often present in peat composts, to judge by the speed at which algae and liverworts sometimes develop on them. Immediately after this watering, clap on the plastic top and leave the pot to drain.

An hour or so later when the pot has cooled down, remove the cover and sow the spores over the surface of the prepared compost. The spores are sure to be packed in an inner envelope. Shake all the spores down to the bottom before opening it. Once it is open, be sure not to sneeze, or you could easily lose the lot! As when sowing seeds, the aim should be to sow the spores as evenly as possible, but you have to rely more on luck than judgement since they are so small you cannot see where they fall. The best one can do is to try and shake them out evenly

Work in a draught free place and scatter the dust-like seeds as evenly as possible.

To ensure it stays moist cover the pot with a plastic dome and keep the saucer full of water.

Once the first fronds appear it is time to give the sporelings more space to prevent overcrowding.

over the whole pot by holding the opened packet at a slight angle and tapping it gently with one finger so that the spores fall out a few at a time. You need to do this in a place where the air is quite still, otherwise the slightest draught could blow away the spores before they even reach the compost.

Having scattered the spores, replace the plastic top, then stand the pot in its saucer and put it where it will be shaded from direct sunlight, such as under the greenhouse staging or on a north-facing windowsill. Finally fill the saucer almost to the brim with water. From then on simply top up the water in the saucer each time it runs low - and have patience. Eventually you will be rewarded by the signs of green growth as the prothali appear. These usually develop until the compost surface

Patch them out by moving small groups into other pots. They can be divided up later if necessary.

is simply covered with them. Continue to top up the saucer as required and leave the pot undisturbed.

A few weeks later you will see that the first fronds of the baby ferns are developing and when they are about ½ in (1 cm) high you can prick them out if you sowed one sort only. But if it was a packet of mixed ferns it is better to wait until you can just distinguish the different kinds, since they do not all develop at the same rate - the reason I am not keen on sowing mixed spores.

At the first move I find it easier to transplant small clusters of the sporelings, as young ferns are called, setting them an inch (2 cm) or so apart in other 5-in (12.5-cm) pots, which are still kept thoroughly moist and covered with domes or plastic bags at first. Later when a little larger, the groups can be split up and planted separately in small pots, though if they are all the same kind there is no reason why two or three should not be grown on together as one plant.

Once they are in their individual pots, keep the compost very moist and the atmosphere about them very humid until the young ferns have had a chance to recover from the move. Then gradually acclimatise them to the ordinary greenhouse or room atmosphere and allow the pots to dry out a little between waterings. From then on they can come under your normal routine care for greenhouse or room plants.

The sort of temperature to aim at during the propagation period depends on the type of ferns you are raising. One of 60F (16C) is ample for hardy ferns, while most of the common greenhouse kinds will do well in a temperature of 65-70F (18-21C).

10. Seed Saving and Storing

To many people, seeds that have never received the benison of having been packeted and paid for cannot be quite 'the real thing'. Yet the plants around us produce countless millions of seeds every year, many of which we call weeds and some we would rather be without. Nonetheless there are innumerable garden plants, trees and shrubs which regularly produce viable seeds and which can be raised from them if anyone cares to gather and sow them. Indeed, in many gardens planted and run on more informal lines, where bare soil and the hoe do not figure to any large degree, a great many seedlings of cultivated plants develop quite naturally. And in a few cases these have resulted in improved forms that are highly prized today.

Whether or not it is worth saving your own seeds rather depends on the plants concerned, because it is very easy to collect seeds that will give you rubbishy plants. But there are cases where it is desirable, if not essential, such as when the life of the seeds is so short that they would be dead before they were sold. There is a strong case also for gathering and immediately sowing the seeds of plants, for example those of some primulas and meconopsis, whose germination becomes inhibited if the seeds are allowed to ripen fully. There is a wide variety of plants in cultivation, seeds of which are not available commercially, that you must gather for yourself or obtain from friends or fellow enthusiasts if you want to raise them. And if you are trying to raise a new or improved variety of any plant you can normally do so only from seed.

Leave Them to Ripen

With a few exceptions it is best to let seeds ripen on the plants before they are gathered, but of course you must take the seedheads before the seeds are shed. This means keeping a careful watch for any changes in the seed vessel or fruit indicating approaching ripeness. Generally seed pods begin to turn brown or black. Experience is the best teacher of the stage at which seeds of different plants are best harvested. Among the trickiest to judge are those of plants that have a mechanism to eject seeds forcefully so that they land some distance away. If you delay too long the seeds can be lost; on the other hand if you pick them too soon the immature seeds may go mouldy or fail to mature. Other plants, like poppies for instance, can still have some seeds in their pods a week or more after they first open.

Where feasible to do so it pays to open a seed head occasionally from plants you are particularly interested in to see how the seeds inside are doing. Once they are brown, gather the heads with a length of stem and place them upside down in paper bags. Do it on a day when the plants are dry and put the bags, which should have the name of the plants written on the outside, in a dry airy place to finish ripening. As the seeds are shed they are contained in the bag. Small plants, like white alyssum, can be pulled up, their roots cut off, then spread on sheets of clean paper in a dry airy place. The seeds fall on to the paper and can be gathered up later to store away. Never use plastic bags when gathering seeds or seed heads since they prevent the plant tissue from drying properly and encourage the growth of moulds.

If gathered before they are fully ripe, seed heads may not open as they should to release their contents. In that case you have no alternative but to break them apart about a fortnight later to extract the seeds. This gives extra work in cleaning the seeds to get rid of the particles of seed pod but is an unavoidable nuisance.

Cleaning Seeds

There are various ways in which dry seeds can be sorted out from rubbish. Large seeds provide little difficulty since they can be picked out individually. With the others, apart from removing large pieces of pod or other debris by hand, some other method must be used. One way is to pass the seeds through two sieves, one having a mesh size that will just pass the seeds, the other being too small. These will get rid of any debris that is larger or smaller than the seeds, but still leaves you with any particles about the same size as the seeds themselves. Few home gardeners are likely to have a suitable selection of sieves, though a flour dredger and fine tea strainer can be helpful.

Another method is a variation of winnowing, where grain is tossed into the air to allow a breeze to blow the lighter chaff to one side. Simply pour the seeds into a basin while blowing very gently through them. An electric fan heater provides a more even air current if you have a lot of seeds to deal with. Another way is to put the seeds in a fairly shallow dish and gently blow to remove any light rubbish. It is wise always to do such cleaning over a large sheet of paper, however, since an over ambitious puff could send the seeds flying too.

Small rounded seeds can often be effectively cleaned quite simply by the aid of a cloth covered board. Simply hold it at an angle just sufficient for the seeds to roll down it, leaving any debris behind.

Seeds contained in fleshy fruits, like a tomato, have to be cleaned before they are dried. Wait until the fruits are really ripe, then scoop out the seeds into a sieve and wash them thoroughly under a running tap to get rid of as much of the pulp as you can. It is impossible to get them completely clean by washing - commercial seed firms use an acid treatment as part of the cleaning process - but this does not matter provided you separate them after washing. Left together they will dry into a solid mass, so space the seeds out on clean sheets of paper and dry them as speedily as possible ready for storage.

Gathering seeds from fruits of the marrow family is similar, except the seeds are large enough to be picked out individually and a quick rinse in running water cleans them quite well. Again dry them as quickly as you can for storing.

Cold Storage

Once clean and dry, the seeds are best put into paper packets or envelopes on which the name and year of collection is clearly marked. From then on their length of life will be largely governed by the way in which they are stored. Seeds survive best when kept dry and cold and the best place for them is in a domestic refrigerator. Many seeds need a further ripening period of several weeks after being gathered in order to complete the embryos, so do not put them into cold storage at once.

As a first step find a suitable-sized tin, jar or plastic box with a well fitting lid. Put your packets of seeds inside it and put it into the refrigerator for 48 hours with the lid open. At the end of this period clap the lid on tight, seal it with plastic adhesive tape and return to the refrigerator. The air in a refrigerator is usually the driest you can find in an ordinary house. It is largely moisture removed from the air, which is changed whenever the refrigerator door is opened, that forms the ice that has to be removed by defrosting from time to time. During the period when the container of seeds is left open, moisture is removed from the seeds and packets themselves, in the same way that it is from uncovered food.

The container is best covered and sealed the first time the refrigerator is opened one morning when it is likely to be at its coldest and driest. If there is room to do so put on the lid before removing the container to seal it. Sealing should help prevent future fluctuation of moisture content. Once prepared in this way the seeds will keep well and even those with a comparatively short life, like delphiniums and scorzonera, should give good germination the following spring.

Chemical Drying

The most effective way of all for drying seeds at home is to make a desiccator, using a large jar or plastic sweet bottle (which can usually be had for the asking from a shop) with a well fitting lid. A large preserving jar fitted with a rubber washer probably gives the best seal but may be rather small for the job. In the base of the container place a tray or bag of silica-gel, a chemical that absorbs moisture from the air. The kind treated with a colour indicator is best. This is pink when dry and blue when charged with moisture. Putting it into a warm oven for a while drives off the moisture to make it pink again and ready for re-use. Your local chemist can usually obtain, if not immediately supply, silica-gel for the purpose.

Having put the chemical dryer into the jar, slip in the packets of seeds and screw down the top. Keep an eye on the colour of the chemical and replace or dry it when it turns blue. The number of times this needs to be done depends on the amount of seeds and the quantity of silica-gel used. Once the colour is stabilised at pink, remove the silica-gel, seal the top of the jar with plastic tape and store in the refrigerator.

The same method can be used to keep opened packets of bought seeds from one season to the next. But there is little point in doing so if you have already left them in a damp shed for months; it is far better to dispose of them and buy fresh seeds for the following year. Many bought seeds are supplied in sealed foil packets these days. These seeds first have their moisture content reduced in a special store and are packeted there as well. As they are sealed in, extra moisture cannot get to them until you open the packet, and they store well in a refrigerator. Once the packet is opened, however, they become as vulnerable to dampness as any other seeds.

One special point to remember is to remove any seed storage container from a refrigerator some hours before opening it. This allows the contents to reach room temperature before coming into contact with the warmer, moister, outside air. If this is not done the seed packets will immediately be dewed with condensation.

It is hardly worth going to such trouble to store seeds of plants that need winter cold to break their dormancy and which are sown in the autumn and left outdoors or in an open cold frame. As I have already explained coldness alone will not do the trick: the seeds must also be charged with moisture.

This type of storage does not suit oily seeds like acorns, conkers and nuts for example. Excessive desiccation can ruin their germinating abilities and the sooner they are sown the better. If they must be stored keep them in damp sand in a cool place.

Stratifying Fruits

Finally there are those seeds contained in fleshy fruits such as rose hips, haws, and holly and yew berries that provide food for birds. Having passed through the digestive tract of a bird they can germinate quite quickly, but when gathered and sown they can take ages. The strange thing about them is that when treated by a process known as stratification - storing the seeds between layers of damp peat or sand for a given period - the germination can be quite even (see page 16). Yet if the seeds are sown immediately and the container exposed to the weather the results can still be very erratic.

The easiest method of stratification for a home gardener is to mix the fruits with damp sand in a plastic bag and bury it in the garden for the required period, remembering, of course, to mark the site plainly with a short stake and label. The stratification period varies, according to species, from six months (covering one winter period) for barberries and roses to 18 months (covering two winter periods) for hawthorn and yews. Stratification saves both space and time that would have to be devoted to the bed or containers were the seeds sown immediately.

What Not to Save

You will notice I have not suggested saving your own seeds as a way to reduce your seed bill. This is because attempts to do so can lead to disaster and prove to be a false economy. The standard seed lines of vegetables and many flowers offered by seed firms are the result of years of care and attention by experts. Great skill is needed to keep such seed lines true to type even after their development. Unless you have some experience it is wiser therefore to buy seeds of these when required. In any case the seed cost per plant produced is so small as to be insignificant in the usual run of flowers and vegetables.

Some plants will breed true from seed, that is produce offspring that are to all intents and purposes the same as themselves; others will not. The difference lies in their genetical make up. Genes are the controllers of inherited characteristics and are present in the cells of all plants. They are spaced along structures called chromosomes which are normally present in a number of pairs. When the gametes, or sex cells are produced these contain only single chromosomes which pair up with those of the other gametes after fertilisation. The cells in a seed therefore contain one set of gene-carrying chromosomes from each parent.

Where the genes of each parent are almost identical there will be little difference between them or their offspring. This is so in the case of most wild plants that grow in our fields and hedgerows where there is little difference between one plant and another of the same species. Very careful inspection will reveal slight irregularities, however, so they are not completely identical. Occasionally there may be a natural mutation that results in a distinct change, perhaps in size or colour of flower, leaf, or complete plant. Whether or not such plants survive in the wild depends on whether they are as well or better adapted to their natural environment and, most important, able to set seeds and breed to increase their kind. Some of the plants in cultivation originated in this way and were noticed and collected by sharp-eyed enthusiasts. It is one reason, also, why many gardeners do take the trouble to raise many less common species from seed. Not only does it provide an opportunity to raise a large number of plants cheaply, but there is always an outside chance that an improved type may turn up.

Hybrid Plants

Where two distinctly different species of the same plant manage to cross pollinate and set seed, the offspring are 'hybrids'. They have a set of genes from each of the two completely different parents and the result can be quite startling. While some of the plants resulting from such a cross may resemble either parent others may be so completely different as to be unrecognisable. Indeed they are completely 'new' plants, though they will still have the same major characteristics that botanists use to identify all members of the genera to which the parents belong.

It is due to such mixed parentage that a great many of our cultivated plants do not breed true to type, and the more mixed their parentage the greater the differences that can arise in each generation as the combination of genes change with each mating.

By a process of cross-breeding and selection, followed by careful work over a number of years to fix the characteristics so that they will breed true to type from one generation to another, plant breeders have created most of the vegetables and ordinary flowers we normally grow from seed. These cultivated varieties - 'cultivators' as they are properly referred to nowadays - may have taken many years to create and great skill and experience is usually needed to bring together the particular qualities aimed for in one plant. But having created it the work still cannot stop, because natural variations could still gradually change the variety until it was unrecognisable from its former self. Consequently mother stock raised to provide each new batch of seed has to be carefully inspected and 'rogue' plants destroyed to keep the variety true to type. Give, say, three experts the job to do, each in a different place, and you will eventually finish up with three stocks of plants which, while still similar, will show minor differences. This is what has deliberately or accidentally given rise to different 'strains' of the same variety, because each expert may have been concentrating on selecting for slightly different characteristics. Thus one could finish up with, say, a larger, and another with an earlier-cropping, strain of cabbage from the original variety.

Although such ordinary varieties may be reliably stable when pollination occurs only between the plants of that particular strain, if you once allow cross pollination with another variety such stability is lost and the following generations of plants can show wide differences. To overcome this seed-producing plants have to be grown well away from any similar plant or isolated in some way to prevent unwanted cross pollination.

The whole process of creating and maintaining seed lines is an expert business and though a few amateurs do manage to keep their own strain of runner beans, onions and leeks going by careful selection each year, and some have raised excellent new varieties of sweet peas, in the majority of cases, and certainly for most gardeners, it is much better to leave it to the experts. In that way you can be sure of raising good plants and not wasting time - possibly a whole season - in growing something that proves to be worthless.

F1 Hybrid Varieties

More and more F1 hybrid varieties have been offered to gardeners over recent years. In the production of these two selected groups of inbred parents are used, one to provide the pollen, the other to produce the seed. The result is progeny that show practically no variation in any form. As well as having the extra vigour that is natural to hybrids, the plants are very even not only in shape, form and colour, but in time of reaching maturity.

These characteristics, while so even in the F1 generation, break up completely in the following one. Consequently any attempt to save seed from such varieties leads to disappointment and seedsmen regularly include warnings in their catalogues against doing so. The same care and attention has to be taken in raising a new batch of parent plants and in repeating the same cross pollination technique each time a fresh lot of F1 hybrid seed is produced, and that is why they tend to be much more expensive.

Moving away from plants commonly raised from seed to perennials that do not breed true to type, there is a greater chance for amateurs to interest themselves in raising something new. Being perennial such plants can usually be propagated by some vegetative means, such as by cuttings or division, to increase their number. This means you need to create only one acceptable plant to begin with and it does not itself have to breed true to type. (Strictly such plants would not form a variety in the botanical sense but are 'clones'. That is every single one has been raised from a piece of another since the original one plant was first produced. Because the genes are the same in the cells, each retains the characteristics of the original plant.)

Many home gardeners get a great deal of interest and satisfaction in raising new dahlias, carnations, large delphiniums, gladioli, auriculas and other flowers. Those magnificent Russell lupins are an example of an amateur's work that completely revolutionised a garden plant and which *could* be raised from seed, though without any certainty of the colour of the flowers. Named forms of a particular colour of these are also clones.

Chances of Success

When dealing with plants of hybrid origin it helps to have some idea of your likely success rate. Some are so mixed that a whole lifetime could be spent on raising failures. Apples, for instance, are a notoriously mixed bunch. The odds of raising an apple equivalent to, let alone better than, Cox's Orange Pippin from a random pip are about 4 million to one against. This is quite apart from the difficulty of getting a quick result, which would involve budding or grafting some wood of the seedling on to a mature tree. A seedling tree could take 15 years or more before it produced a single fruit.

The difficulties in raising a worthwhile variety of many garden plants from seed is nowhere near as great as I have suggested for apples. And your chances of success will be much better still if you have a basic understanding of simple genetics. If you know how heredity factors are controlled you can shorten the odds considerably by carefully recording what you do and the results you get, as well as planning what crosses to make. But first you have to decide on what it is you are aiming for. It may be that you want larger or more flowers on a plant, greater weather resistance, more compact growth or some other attribute. Where a specially required characteristic appears in one variety, even if an inferior kind, it may be possible to join it with those of another favoured variety by crossing the two.

How Genes Work

I have already mentioned genes, or heredity factor controllers, which are present on a number of pairs of chromosomes in each cell nucleus. Also that only one set of chromosomes is present in each gamete, or sex cell, which pair off on fertilisation. In this way each new individual will have a representative sample of the genes of both its parents, which will control its growth and behaviour. Genes do not work in isolation, however, but in conjunction. Some tend to override the effects of others and are said to be dominant. When these are present their effect is always uppermost. If these are removed by breeding, however, the less powerful, recessive genes are allowed to work and so you may get a different type of plant.

It will no doubt be easier to understand if we look at a simple example. Let us suppose we have a red-flowered plant. It has on both chromosomes of one pair a gene R responsible for the red colouring. We also have a white-flowered variety with the gene W controlling its petal colour. If we cross pollinate these two plants each will provide one set of chromosomes so each offspring will receive genes R and W:

RR x WW

♦

RW RW

The effect this will have on the new seedlings' flowers will depend on whether or not one of these genes is dominant. If it is this will override the other and so all the flowers will be red or white. Should they be more or less equally matched we may find that the flowers are pink instead.

This first generation is known as the F1 (or first filial) generation. If we then cross these F1 plants to produce an F2 (or second filial) generation, the offspring will be mixed, because each parent may provide one or other of the two genes on the single set of chromosomes in the gametes. Consequently the F2 plant may contain genes in the following combinations:

RW x RW

♦

RR RW WR WW

Where the red gene is dominant, only one plant would have white flowers: that with the WW combination.

To distinguish between dominant and recessive genes, the dominant ones only are given a capital letter. It is customary, too, for the genes from the male, or pollen providing parent, to be put in brackets. Thus the F1 cross with a dominant red gene would be:

R w x (R)(w)

R(R) R(w) w(R) w(w)

Let us now consider a case involving two factors by allowing for height as well as flower colour. Supposing the red plant was tall due to gene T and the white plant short with gene S. The result of crossing them would be:

RR TT x (ww)(ss)

R(w)T(s) R(w)T(s)

If we then went on to the F2 generation it is easier to work out the combinations in a diagrammatic table.

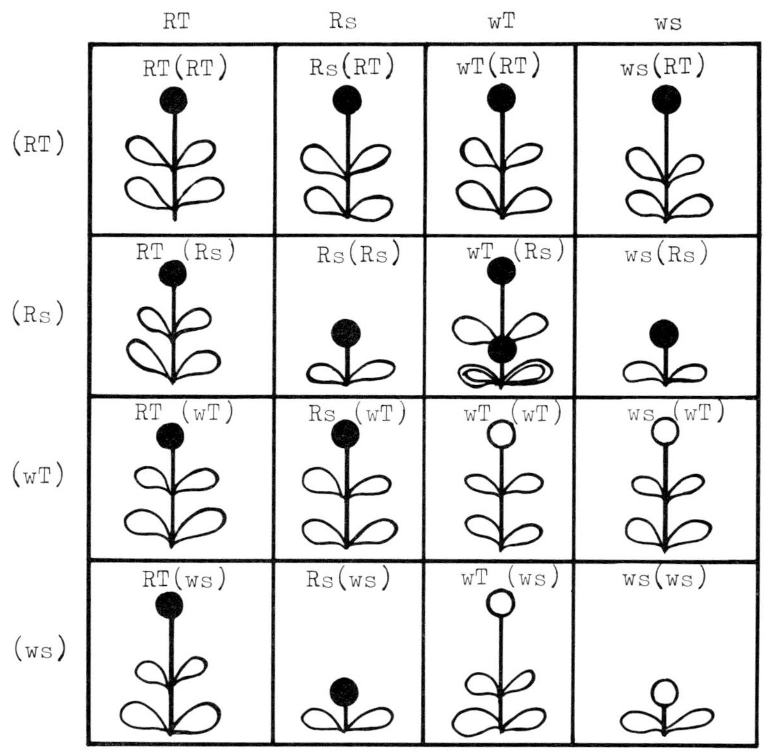

As you can see the result is predominantly tall red plants, but there are three tall white and three short red ones as well. What is more, only two (top left and bottom right) are genetically the same as the original parents. This is a very simplified example, of course, but serves to demonstrate two important points. New mixtures of genes are created in the F1 generation, but these may show little or no variation. It is when these in turn are selfed (self-pollinated) and crossed among themselves that the genes are sorted into a rich variety of combinations and give rise to the widest differences. This is why most breeders always work at least to the F2 generation, even if the plant they were aiming for turned up as an F1 plant.

These examples also assume that the genes on each chromosome of a pair in the original parents are the same. A great many garden plants are themselves hybrids, however, so their genes are likely to be very mixed to begin with. The result is that even first generation plants can show a lot of variation, which increases in the F2 generation.

Linked Characteristics

In addition, although the genes transferred to the gametes are taken randomly from either chromosome of each pair to make up the number, some tend to move in groups so that the same characteristics tend to appear together when inherited. Thus strong scent may only appear with, say, red flowers. Such genes are said to be 'linked' and it may take a great deal of work to break such a linkage. Indeed splitting them up may prove to be an insoluble problem.

Genes are also affected by their neighbours, even by their position on the chromosome, so a large number of genes may directly or indirectly have a hand in controlling certain inherited traits.

It is sensible, therefore, to keep detailed records of your own work when breeding plants. This can show where plants are likely to hold the characteristics you are looking for and, most important, are able to pass them on to their offspring. You can save a lot of work, too, if you take the trouble to read any published information about what other people have already tried or achieved. A full study of genetics is beyond the scope of this book and, if you become seriously interested in plant breeding, it is worth reading one or two of the specialist volumes devoted to the subject.

Selective Breeding

The most elementary method of selective cross breeding is simply to grow together plants of the same type in a bed and save and grow the seeds they produce. However, if you do obtain a reasonable plant and would like to try and improve it further you have no way of knowing which plants were the parents. There may even be factors which prevent cross pollination at all. Some flowers may be self-fertile and pollinate themselves. Other plants may not flower at the right time to enable them to cross pollinate, or be completely sterile. You need to know something about the plants to begin with if you intend to breed selectively.

The obvious way is first to pick closely related plants or varieties that show evidence of the characteristics you wish to try and combine. These should then be carefully cross pollinated, using the pollen from one to fertilise several flowers of the other and vice versa. Each flower head should be tagged with a reference number and full details entered in a record book. The same reference number should be used to mark the packets the seeds are eventually stored in and to label the boxes or seed rows when they are eventually sown. Notes of such things as harvesting and sowing dates and germination performance, as well as the eventual results, should also be recorded for future reference.

Merely transferring pollen between the flowers is not enough, however, if you want to be sure that the crosses are true. You have to ensure that the pollen gathered is the right kind by preventing insects from bringing in and mixing strange pollen with it. This can be done by enclosing the buds in paper bags or fine nylon material before they open. You should also make sure that the seed bearing plant cannot be either cross pollinated by visiting insects, or self pollinated with its own pollen. The first can be prevented again by enclosing the flower within a paper bag: the second by emasculating the bloom and removing the stamens before the anthers at their tips are ripe enough to shed their pollen. A few plants, like those of the marrow family, conveniently carry the male and female organs in separate flowers; others, like some hollies and *Viburnum davidii*, have all male or all female flowers on different plants. But the majority of plants will need special treatment to avoid self pollination.

Transferring the Pollen

The pollen grains can be transferred with the aid of a small, soft paint brush, which must be washed in spirits and dried again after each use to clean it. Alternatively the rough torn edge of a strip of fibrous paper, which can be discarded after a single use, will do. The best time to carry out pollination is when the stigma is receptive and, usually, sticky. Then the pollen sticks to it readily and soon germinates. Each pollen grain develops a tube which grows down the style to the ovary cavity where fertilisation then occurs.

Pollen grains from different plants vary considerably in their length of life. Some can be stored for weeks in dry air at a temperature near freezing, which can enable plants that flower at completely different times to be crossed.

After pollination, keep the treated flowers covered for a few days until they are no longer receptive. A withering of the style and swelling of the ovary are signs that this is so. Then any protective covering should be removed and the seed head left to develop and ripen naturally. It is wise to remove the faded petals if they do not drop off. Left on they could rot and infect the seed head and spoil your chances of getting any seeds. It is also sensible to remove any other flowers or buds not required for pollination in order to concentrate the plant's energies into plumping up those special seed heads.

Later check the seed vessels for the first signs of ripening. It is all too easy to lose the seeds due to their being shed before you expect it, which could waste a whole season's work. If necessary, cover them with muslin or paper bags to prevent accidents. Otherwise follow the procedures I have already suggested for saving and storing seeds.

Although most breeding work is carried on out of doors there is a distinct advantage in growing small plants in pots in a greenhouse for the purpose, especially half-hardy plants like petunias, that need more warmth to seed freely. It is also much easier to work on them there as well as to check that cross pollination has been successful and to protect the ripening seed pods.

Choosing Wild Plants

Conservationists have popularised the idea of growing wild plants in recent years and many of these are often no more difficult to grow from seed than cultivated ones. Although the movement is chiefly concerned with the protection of species that are fast disappearing, a large number of 'wildings' have always been popular with a select band of enthusiasts who recognise the garden value of such native plants as common foxgloves, harebells, marsh marigolds and cowslips. A single seed head of commoner plants pocketed during a country ramble will generally give sufficient seedlings to satisfy the average gardener, and there are now several firms specialising in the supply of seeds of a very wide range of wild plants, including quite rare species.

Just because native species thrive in the wild, however, it does not follow that they will grow even better in a garden. Those that are to be found only in particular areas can be difficult. They are localised because they need certain conditions of soil or climate. A plant from chalk downs is unlikely to do well in acid soil for instance: nor is a stream-side native likely to be happy in a dry, sandy plot. It may therefore be necessary to adapt the site to suit such plants.

Beware, also, of introducing perpetual weeds. Scarlet corn poppies may look bright along the bank of a motorway, and the stately rosebay willowherb can make a startling patch of colour in midsummer; but both can run riot in a plot by seeding themselves furiously over any patch of bare soil. Treat with caution, too, plants like the scented winter heliotrope, *Petasites fragrans*, which is a rampant ground coverer and extremely difficult to be rid of once it is established.

Seed Testing

There are inevitably times when it pays to test the germination of seeds to see if they are worth sowing. It may be that you have some that you have carefully saved for a year or even two that you want to make use of, or some that you have gathered for yourself. Although you will eventually find out after sowing them, a failure may upset your cropping plans in a vegetable garden or, in the case of flowers, be discovered too late to obtain fresh seed and sow another batch for that season.

Germination failures can also be due to reasons other than poor seed. If you did not test the seeds first you cannot then be sure exactly what was the cause. Although people tend to blame seed for such troubles, the real problem is often allowing the soil to dry out at a critical time, sowing too deeply or in ground that is too wet and cold, or allowing slugs to attack. If you can rule out the seeds as a possible cause to begin with, therefore, you then know you must re-examine your sowing technique if failure occurs.

Testing the germinating power of seeds is easily done a few weeks ahead of sowing. Use a clean saucer or plastic lid of suitable size and cover it with a thickness or two of absorbent paper. Filter paper (which can be bought from most home-brewing and wine-making shops) is best, especially for tiny seeds, since it contains no harmful chemicals, but a double thickness of paper kitchen towelling seems to work well with most seeds. Thoroughly moisten the paper then space out a chosen number of seeds on it, preferably ten or more. The larger the number the more accurate the result will be. Cover the seeds with a transparent lid - an upturned tumbler will do - then put them in a suitably warm place and keep them moist. The time needed for the seeds to shoot can vary from 2-28 days, most common vegetables and flowers taking about 10. At the end of that time check on the number that have germinated and work out the percentage. A germination rate of one in ten seeds represents 10%. If the rate is below 20%, unless it is seed of a rare species or a plant you know to be difficult, discard it and obtain some more.

Loss of Vigour

An important point you should always bear in mind when deciding whether or not to use a batch of saved seed is the fact that old seeds frequently have less vigour than new ones. They may germinate quite well under test conditions, but the success rate can be cut by half, or even more when they are sown under less than ideal conditions out of doors. Remember, too, that not all seeds that germinate necessarily produce good plants. Some may be malformed and useless. For this reason you should in any case expect to increase the number of seeds sown. It is for these reasons that I do not advocate saving packeted seeds from one year to the next. Most gardeners will enjoy far greater success by using fresh seeds wherever possible.

This method of testing seeds cannot be used without some adaptation for any which have germination inhibitors. Beetroot, for instance, need to be soaked in several changes of water for 24 hours to get rid of a chemical inhibitor. Those, like eryngiums, that need a period of cold to trigger growth, should be started off in plastic boxes and put in a refrigerator for three weeks. At the end of this time give them warmth to see if any germinate. If there is still no sign of growth, a second and perhaps even a third cold period may be needed to start them off. To deal with some of the most difficult seeds, commercial firms use special chemicals to test whether the seeds are actually viable, but this is not practicable in the home.

A further point to remember when testing home-saved seeds is that many require a further ripening period after being gathered before they will attempt to germinate. It is no good testing them at once, therefore. Unless you have a special reason for needing to check their viability earlier, leave the testing until about a month before they are due to be sown.

Appendices

Appendix 1:
Sowing Suggestions and Germination Times for Ornamental Plants†

Name[1]	Sow in autumn or pre-chill[2]	Pre-soak and/or chip seeds[3]	Germination temperature °F(C)[4]	Time taken to germinate[5]	Leave seeds uncovered[6]	Remarks
Aubitilon HHSh		★	65-70(18-21)	M		
Acacia HHS		★	65-80(18-27)	M		
Acanthus HP			50-55(10-13)	M		
Achillea HP			65-70(18-21)	S/VS	★	Erratic†
Achimines GP			65-80(18-27)	M/S	★	Mix with sand
Aconitum HP	★		55-60(10-13)	S/VS	★	Erratic
Acroclinium HA			60-70(16-21)	M		
Agapanthus HHBb			60-65(16-18)	S		
Agastache HP			55-60(13-18)	M		
Agave HP			55-60(13-16)	S	★	Erratic
Ageratum HHA			65-75(18-21)	Q		
Agrostemma HA			55-60(13-16)	M		
Ailanthus HT	★	★	55-60(13-16)	S		Erratic
Alchemilla HP			60-65(16-18)	M		
Allium HBb	★		55-60(13-16)	S/VS	★	Erratic
Aloe GP			65-70(18-21)	S/VS	★	
Alstroemeria HP		★	65-75(18-24)	S/VS		Erratic. Sow singly in pots to avoid root disturbance
Alyssum HA,HP			55-70(13-21)	M	★	Barely cover seeds when sown outdoors

† See Footnotes on page 190 for abbreviations, etc.

Name[1]	Sow in autumn or pre-chill[2]	Pre-soak and/or chip seeds[3]	Germination temperature °F(C)[4]	Time taken to germinate[5]	Leave seeds uncovered[6]	Remarks
Amaranthus HHA			70-80(21-27)	M		
Amaranthus HA			60-70(16-21)	M		Tiny seeds - keep seeds moist until seedlings appear
Amaryllis GBb			65-70(18-21)	M/S		Keep tiny bulbs growing over first winter. Erratic
Anagallis HHA			50-65(10-18)	M/S		
Anaphalis HP			55-65(13-18)	M		
Anchusa HA, HP			65-80(18-27)	M		
Antennaria HP			55-60(13-16)	M/S		
Anthemis HP			65-70(18-21)	Q	★	
Antirrhinum HHA			65-80(18-27)	M		Barely cover seeds
Aquilegia HP	★		65-70(18-21)	M/S		Can be erratic
Arabis HP			65-70(18-21)	M		Barely cover seeds
Aralia GP			65-75(18-24)	M		
Arbutus HT	★		65-70(18-21)	S	★	Erratic
Arctotis HHA			60-70(16-21)	M/S		
Arenaria HP			55-65(13-18)	M	★	
Argemone HA			60-70(16-21)	M		
Armeria HP			60-70(16-21)	M		
Arum HP			55-65(13-18)	S/VS		
Aruncus HP			55-65(13-18)	S		
Asparagus GP		★	65-80(18-27)	M		
Asphodelus HP			65-70(18-21)	M		

Name[1]	Sow in autumn or pre-chill[2]	Pre-soak and/or chip seeds[3]	Germination temperature °F(C)[4]	Time taken to germinate[5]	Leave seeds uncovered[6]	Remarks
Aster HHA			65-70(18-21)	Q		
Aster HP	★		60-70(16-21)	M		Erratic
Astilbe	★		60-65(13-18)	S	★	
Astrantia HP			55-65(13-18)	S/VS	★	Erratic
Aubretia HP			60-70(16-21)	M	★	
Auricula HP			60-70(16-21)	M/S		Erratic. Keep compost moist
Azalea HSh	★		55-65(13-18)	S	★	Erratic. Shade seedlings from direct sunlight
Balsam HHA			65-80(18-27)	M		
Bartonia HA			55-65(13-18)	M		
Begonia HHA			65-80(18-27)	S/VS	★	Mix seed with sand. Shade seedlings from bright sun
Bellis HB			65-70(18-21)	M		
Beloperone GP			65-75(18-24)	S/VS	★	Erratic
Berberis HSh	★		55-65(13-18)	VS	★	Erratic
Bergenia HP	★		60-70(16-21)	S/VS	★	
Betula HT	★		65-70(18-21)	S	★	Erratic
Bletilla HHP			65-70(18-21)	S/VS	★	Erratic
Brachycombe HHA			65-80(18-27)	M		Barely cover seeds
Briza HA			60-75(16-24)	M		
Browallia GP			60-65(16-18)	M	★	
Brunfelsia GP			65-80(18-27)	S		
Buddelia HSh	★		65-75(18-21)	M/S		

Name[1]	Sow in autumn or pre-chill[2]	Pre-soak and/or chip seeds[3]	Germination temperature °F(C)[4]	Time taken to germinate[5]	Leave seeds uncovered[6]	Remarks
Buphthalmum HP			70-75(21-24)	M	★	
Cacalia HHP			60-70(16-21)	M		
Cacti and Succulents HHP			60-70(16-21)	Q/VS	★	Shade seedlings from direct sun. Erratic
Calandrinia HHA			55-60(13-16)	Q/M		
Calceolaria HHP, GP			65-70(18-21)	M	★	Grow on seedlings in cool conditions
Calendula HA			60-65(16-18)	M		
Calliopsis HA			60-65(16-18)	M		
Camellia HSh	★	★	70-80(21-27)	S		
Campanula HB, HP			60-70(16-21)	M	★	
Canna HHP		★	65-80(18-27)	M/S		Sow in small pots to avoid root disturbance
Capsicum GA			65-80(18-27)	M	★	
Cardiocrinum HP	★		50-60(10-16)	VS		
Caryipteris HSh			65-75(18-24)	S		Erratic
Catalpa HT			65-70(18-21)	M	★	
Catananche HP			60-70(16-21)	M		
Ceanothus HSh	★	★	65-70(18-21)	S	★	
Cedrus HT	★	★	60-65(16-18)	M/S	★	Erratic
Celosia HHA			65-80(18-27)	Q		Keep moist
Celsia HHP			55-65(13-18)	Q		
Centauria HA, HP			60-75(16-24)	Q/M		

Name[1]	Sow in autumn or pre-chill[2]	Pre-soak and/or chip seeds[3]	Germination temperature °F(C)[4]	Time taken to germinate[5]	Leave seeds uncovered[6]	Remarks
Cerastium HP			60-70(16-21)	Q		
Cercis HSh	★	★	65-75(18-24)	S		Erratic
Chaenomeles HSh	★		55-65(13-18)	S	★	Erratic
Chamaecyparis HT	★		60-70(16-21)	S	★	Erratic
Cheiranthus HB			65-75(18-24)	Q		Raise in outdoor seedbed
Chelone HP			55-65(13-18)	M/S		Do not overwater
Chimonanthes HSh	★		55-60(13-16)	S	★	Erratic
Chionodoxa HBb			55-60(13-16)	S		Erratic
Chrysanthemum HA, HP			60-70(16-21)	M		
Cimicifuga HP			55-60(13-16)	S/VS		Erratic
Cineraria GA			50-60(10-16)	M		Keep seedlings cool
Circium HP			65-70(18-21)	M		
Cistus HSh			65-80(18-27)	M/S		Erratic. Barely cover seeds. Can respond to pre-cooling
Cladanthus HA			60-70(16-21)	M		
Clarkia HA			60-80(16-27)	M		Best sown where to flower
Clematis HSh	★		68-75(20-24)	S/VS		Erratic. Barely cover seeds
Cleome HHA			65-80 (18-27)	M	★	Warmth essential
Clivia GP			80-85(27-30)	M		Seeds short lived
Cobaea HHA		★	65-80(18-27)	M		Can fail at lower temp.
Coffea GSh		★	80-85(27-30)	S		Erratic. Remove seed coats after soaking

Name[1]	Sow in autumn or pre-chill[2]	Pre-soak and/or chip seeds[3]	Germination temperature °F(C)[4]	Time taken to germinate[5]	Leave seeds uncovered[6]	Remarks
Coleus HHP			65-80(18-27)	M	★	Sensitive to high and low temp.
Colutea HSh		★	60-70(16-21)	M		
Convallaria HP	★		50-60(10-16)	S/VS		May need two chilling periods to break double dormancy
Convolvulus HA		★	65-80(18-27)	Q		
Cordyline GP		★	65-80(18-27)	S		Erratic
Coreopsis HP			60-70(16-21)	M		Barely cover seeds
Cortaderia HP			65-80(18-27)	M	★	Warmth essential
Cosmea HHA			65-80(18-27)	Q		
Cotoneaster HSh, HT			65-70(18-21)	VS		Erratic. Barely cover seeds. Needs warm then cold period to trigger germination
Crepis HA			65-80(18-27)	M		Barely cover seeds
Crossandra GP			65-80(18-27)	M	★	Erratic
Cuphea HHP			65-80(18-27)	M	★	Erratic
Cyclamen GP		★	65-70(18-21)	M/S		Keep moist and dark
Cyclamen HP	★		60-65(16-18)	S/VS		Keep moist and dark
Cynoglossum HA			65-80(18-27)	Q		
Cyperus HHP			65-75(18-24)	M		Barely cover seeds
Cytisus HSh		★	65-75(18-24)	M		Erratic. Sow shallowly in individual pots
Dahlia HHA, HHP			65-80(18-27)	Q/M		Keep permanently moist

Name[1]	Sow in autumn or pre-chill[2]	Pre-soak and/or chip seeds[3]	Germination temperature °F(C)[4]	Time taken to germinate[5]	Leave seeds uncovered[6]	Remarks
Daphne HSh	★		50-60(10-16)	VS	★	Erratic. Summer sow in frame: needs warm followed by cold period to trigger germination
Datura GSh			55-65(13-18)	M/S		
Delphinium HA			55-65(13-18)	Q		Keep moist. High temp. can cause failure
Delphinium HP	★		55-65(13-18)	M		Best autumn sown. Badly stored seeds soon lose viability
Dianthus HA, HP			60-70(16-21)	Q/M		Broken seeds can give malformed seedlings
Diascia GA			60-65(16-18)	M		
Dictamnus HP	★		60-70(16-21)	S/VS		Erratic
Didiscus GA			60-70(16-21)	M		Keep moist
Dierama HP			60-65(16-18)	S/VS	★	Erratic
Digitalis HB, HP			65-80(18-27)	M	★	Keep moist
Dimorphotheca HHA			60-70(16-21)	Q		Barely cover seeds
Dipsacus HB			65-80(18-27)	Q/M		Sow where to grow
Dodecatheon HP	★		65-70(18-21)	VS		Erratic
Dolichos HHA		★	65-70(18-21)	M		
Dononicum HP			65-70(18-21)	M	★	
Dracaena GSh			75-85(24-30)	S/VS	★	Erratic - keep just moist
Dracunculus HP			55-70(13-21)	S/VS		Erratic - keep just moist
Dryas HP	★		60-70(16-21)	S/VS		Erratic

Name[1]	Sow in autumn or pre-chill[2]	Pre-soak and/or chip seeds[3]	Germination temperature °F(C)[4]	Time taken to germinate[5]	Leave seeds uncovered[6]	Remarks
Eccremocarpus HHP			65-70(18-21)	S		Barely cover seeds
Echinops HP			65-80(18-27)	M/S		Easily raised out of doors
Echium HA			60-70(16-21)	Q		Best sown where to flower
Episcia GP			65-80(18-27)	M/S	★	Mix seeds with sand
Eranthis HBb	★		60-70(16-21)	S/VS		Erratic
Eremurus HP			55-65(13-18)	S/VS		Erratic. Barely cover seeds
Erica HSh	★		60-70(16-21)	S	★	Erratic. Use lime-free compost
Erigeron HP			65-70(18-21)	M	★	
Erinus HP			65-75(18-24)	M	★	
Eryngium HP	★		65-70 (18-21)	M/S	★	Erratic. May need several periods of artificial chilling to trigger germination
Erythrina HHSh		★	65-80(18-27)	Q/M		
Eschscholtzia HA			60-70(16-21)	M		Seedlings resent root disturbance
Exacum GA			65-70(18-21)	M	★	Mix with sand
Fagus HT	★	★	55-60(13-16)	S/VS		Erratic
Fatsia HHSh			65-80(18-27)	M		Avoid overwatering
Felicia HHA			65-70(18-21)	M		Barely cover seeds
Ficus GP			70-80(21-27)	M/S	★	
Forsythia HSh			55-60(13-16)	S		
Francoa HHP			50-55(10-13)	M	★	
Freesia HHBb		★	60-70(16-21)	M		Grow on seedlings outdoors in summer

Name[1]	Sow in autumn or pre-chill[2]	Pre-soak and/or chip seeds[3]	Germination temperature °F(C)[4]	Time taken to germinate[5]	Leave seeds uncovered[6]	Remarks
Fuchsia GP			65-80(18-27)	M/S	★	Erratic
Gaillardia HHA, HP			65-70(18-21)	M	★	
Galtonia HBb			65-75(18-24)	M/S		Erratic
Gardenia HSh			65-75(18-24)	M		Use lime-free compost
Gaultheria HSh	★		65-70(18-21)	S		Use lime-free compost
Gazania HHA			65-80(18-27)	M		
Gentiana HP	★		60-65(16-18)	M/VS		Erratic. Use lime-free compost. Keep pots over at least two winters for late germination
Geranium HP	★		50-60(10-16)	S		Erratic. Barely cover seeds
Gerbera GP			65-70(18-21)	Q/M		Seed short lived. Sow seeds pointed end down, burying to half their length Grow on in cool conditions
Gesnaria GP			65-75(18-24)	Q/M	★	
Geum HP			65-80(18-27)	M/S		Erratic
Gilia HHA			65-70(18-21)	M		
Gingko HT	★		65-75(18-24)	S		Erratic. Barely cover seeds
Glaucium HA			60-65 (16-18)	M		Best sown where to flower
Gomphocarpus GP			65-75(18-24)	M		
Globularia HP	★		55-60(13-16)	M	★	
Gloxinia GP			65-75(18-24)	M	★	Pot-off seedlings when second leaves begin to form
Godetia HA			60-70(16-21)	Q		Best sown where to flower

Name[1]	Sow in autumn or pre-chill[2]	Pre-soak and/or chip seeds[3]	Germination temperature °F(C)[4]	Time taken to germinate[5]	Leave seeds uncovered[6]	Remarks
Gomphrena HHA			65-80(18-27)	Q		
Gossypium GA			65-75(18-24)	M		
Gourds HHA			65-85(18-30)	M		Sow in individual pots
Grasses HA, HHA, HP			60-80(16-27)	M/S		Lightly cover seeds sown in open ground
Grevillea HHSh		★	65-80(18-27)	M	★	
Gunnera HP			70-80(21-27)	M/S		Erratic
Gymnocladus HT		★	65-75(18-24)	S		Erratic
Gypsophila HA, HP			60-70(16-21)	M		
Hamamelis HSh	★		55-60(13-16)	VS		Erratic. Barely cover seeds. Needs warm period followed by cold to trigger germination
Hedychium HHP		★	65-80(18-27)	M		
Helenium HP			65-70(18-21)	Q		
Helianthemum HP			65-75(18-24)	M	★	Keep moist. Chill if no seedlings appear in 3 months
Helianthus HA			65-80(18-27)	Q		
Helichrysum HHA			65-85(18-30)	Q	★	Barely cover seeds sown in open ground. Keep moist
Heliopsis HP			65-70(18-21)	Q		
Heliotropium HHP			65-80(18-27)	M/S		Erratic
Helipterum HA			65-75(18-24)	M		
Helleborus HP	★		60-70(18-21)	S/VS		Erratic. May need repeat chilling

Name[1]	Sow in autumn or pre-chill[2]	Pre-soak and/or chip seeds[3]	Germination temperature °F(C)[4]	Time taken to germinate[5]	Leave seeds uncovered[6]	Remarks
Hemerocallis HP	★		60-70(16-21)	S/VS		Erratic
Heracleum HP	★		55-60(13-16)	S		
Heucher HP			60-75(16-21)	M/S	★	
Hibiscus GA			65-70(18-21)	M		
Hollyhock HP			60-75(16-24)	Q	★	
Hosta HP			50-60(10-16)	S		Erratic
Hunnemannia HHA			65-80(18-27)	M		
Hypericum HSh			60-80(16-27)	S		Erratic
Hypoestes GP			65-80(18-27)	Q		
Iberis HA, HP			65-80(18-27)	Q/M		Perennials can be erratic
Impatiens HHA, GP			70-75(21-24)	M	★	Erratic. Germinate in even temp. and good light. Cover pots with plastic to maintain humidity
Incarvillea HP			60-70(16-21)	M	★	
Indigofera HHSh		★	50-60(10-16)	S		Erratic
Inula HP			55-65(13-18)	M/S		
Ipomoea HHA		★	70-85(21-30)	Q/M		Sow in individual pots
Iris HP	★		60-70(16-21)	S/VS		Erratic. May need double chilling
Jacaranda GSh			65-80(18-27)	M		
Jacobaea HA			65-80(18-27)	Q/M		
Jacobinia GP		★	70-85(21-30)	S/VS		Erratic

Name[1]	Sow in autumn or pre-chill[2]	Pre-soak and/or chip seeds[3]	Germination temperature °F(C)[4]	Time taken to germinate[5]	Leave seeds uncovered[6]	Remarks
Jasminum HSh			70-75(21-24)	M		Erratic
Juniperus HSh		★	50(10)	S/VS		Erratic. Winter sow. Excessive warmth can inhibit germination. Barely cover seeds
Kalanchoe GP			70-80(21-27)	Q/M	★	Erratic
Kniphofia HP			65-85(18-30)	M		Easily raised outdoors
Kochia HHA			65-70(18-21)	Q	★	Old seed may not germinate at high temperature
Lamium HP			60-70(16-21)	S		Erratic. Barely cover seeds
Lantana HHP		★	65-80(18-27)	S		Erratic
Larix HT	★		60-70(16-21)	S		Erratic. Barely cover seeds
Lathyrus HA		★	55-65(13-18)	M		Sow in individual pots or where to flower. Do not chip pale coloured seeds
Lathyrus HP		★	55-65(13-18)	M/VS		Erratic. Sow in pots to avoid pricking out
Lavatera HA			65-70(18-21)	M		
Lavendula HSh	★		60-70(16-21)	M/S		Erratic. High temperature may inhibit germination
Layia HA			65-70(18-21)	M		
Leontopodium HP	★		55-70(13-21)	M/S	★	Mix seeds with sand
Leptosiphon HA			55-65(13-18)	M		Best sown where to flower

Name[1]	Sow in autumn or pre-chill[2]	Pre-soak and/or chip seeds[3]	Germination temperature °F(C)[4]	Time taken to germinate[5]	Leave seeds uncovered[6]	Remarks
Lewisia HP	★		50-60(10-16)	VS	★	Erratic. Can take over a year to germinate
Liatris HP			60-80(16-27)	M		Easily raised outdoors
Ligularia HP			60-70(16-21)	M/S	★	Erratic
Lilium	★†		65-75(18-24)	S/VS	★†	Erratic†. Sow seeds on edge († According to species)
Limnanthes HA			55-65(13-18)	M		Best sown where to flower
Linaria HA			55-70(13-21)	M		Barely cover seeds
Linum HA, HP			60-70(16-21)	M		Easily raised outdoors
Lobelia HHA			65-80(18-27)	M	★	Mix seeds with sand
Lobelia HHP	★		65-80(18-27)	S	★	Erratic
Lonas HA			60-70(16-21)	Q		
Lunaria HB			60-70(16-21)	Q		
Lupinus HP		★	60-70(15-21)	M/S		Erratic
Lychnis HP			60-70(16-21)	M	★	Chilling may improve
Lysimachia HP			60-65(16-18)	S	★	Erratic
Lythrum HP			65-70(18-21)	M		
Mahonia HSh	★		50-60(10-16)	VS		Erratic
Malope HA			65-70(18-21)	M		
Malva HP			65-70(18-21)	Q/M		
Malus HT	★	★	50-55(10-13)	VS		Erratic
Matricaria HP			60-70(18-21)	M/VS		Erratic. Barely cover the seeds
Matricaria HHA			65-70(18-21)	Q/M	★	

Name[1]	Sow in autumn or pre-chill[2]	Pre-soak and/or chip seeds[3]	Germination temperature °F(C)[4]	Time taken to germinate[5]	Leave seeds uncovered[6]	Remarks
Matthiola HHA			55-70(13-21)	Q		Keep moist
Meconopsis HP	★		55-70(13-21)	M/S	★	Erratic
Mesembryanthemum HHA			65-70(18-21)	M		Barely cover seeds and germinate in darkness
Microsperma GA			60-70(16-21)	Q		
Mimosa GP		★	70-80(21-27)	M		
Mimulus HHP	★		65-70(18-21)	Q/M	★	
Mirabilis HHA			65-70(18-21)	Q/M	★	
Mina HHA			65-70(18-21)	M/S		Sow in individual pots
Molucella HHA			70-80(21-27)	M		Erratic. Barely cover seeds. Do not sow early outdoors
Monarda HP			60-70(16-21)	M/S		
Monstera GP			65-75(18-24)	M	★	
Morus HT	★		65-70(18-21)	M		Erratic. Barely cover seeds
Musa GP			65-70(18-21)	M		Sow in individual pots
Myosotis HB			65-70(18-21)	M		Barely cover seeds
Myrtus HHSh		★	65-75(18-24)	M		Erratic
Nasturtium HA			65-70(18-21)	Q/M		Best sown where to flower. Avoid sowing early
Nemesia HHA			55-65(13-18)	M	★	
Nemophila HA			55-60(13-16)	M		Sow early where to flower. High temp. may inhibit germination

Name[1]	Sow in autumn or pre-chill[2]	Pre-soak and/or chip seeds[3]	Germination temperature °F(C)[4]	Time taken to germinate[5]	Leave seeds uncovered[6]	Remarks
Nepeta HP			65-70(18-21)	M		
Nerine HHBb			65-70(18-21)	M	★	Seeds soon lose viability. Keep moist
Nertera GP			70-75(21-24)	S	★	Erratic. Mix seed with sand. Seedlings need high humidity
Nicandra HA			60-70(16-21)	M		
Nicotiana HHA			65-80(18-27)	M		Barely cover seeds
Nirembergia HHP			65-80(18-27)	M		
Nigella HA			65-75(18-24)	Q		Best sown where to flower. Keep soil moist
Nolana HHA			65-75(18-24)	M		
Ocimum HHA			55-65(13-18)	M/S	★	
Oenothera HB, HP			65-80(18-27)	M		
Omphalodes HP			60-70(16-21)	M/S		
Onopordon HB, HP			55-65(13-18)	S		
Oxalis HBb			55-65(13-18)	S		
Paeonia HP	★		55-60(13-16)	V		Erratic. Barely cover seeds, shade seedlings from sun
Papaver HA			60-65(16-18)	M		Best sown shallowly where to flower
Papaver HP			60-65(16-18)	M	★	Best raised in individual pots to avoid pricking out
Passiflora HHP		★	65-80(18-27)	S/VS		Erratic. Keep moist

Name[1]	Sow in autumn or pre-chill[2]	Pre-soak and/or chip seeds[3]	Germination temperature °F(C)[4]	Time taken to germinate[5]	Leave seeds uncovered[6]	Remarks
Pelargonium HHP			70-75(21-24)	Q		Use well-drained compost. Germinate in even temp.
Pentas GP			70-80(21-27)	M	★	
Pentstemon HHP			70-80(21-27)	M		Chilling may improve germination
Peperomia GP			65-80(18-27)	M	★	
Perilla HHA			70-80(21-27)	M	★	
Petunia HHA			70-75(21-24)	M	★	
Phacelia HA			55-70(13-21)	M		Best sown where to flower
Philodendron GP			70-80(21-27)	M/VS	★	Erratic. Shade seedlings from direct sun
Phlox HHA			60-65(16-18)	M		
Phlox HP	★		60-70(16-21)	M		Erratic. Keep moist
Pheonix GP			70-80(21-27)	S		Erratic
Phormium HP			60-70(16-21)	S/VS		Erratic
Phygelius HHP			65-80(18-27)	Q		
Physalis HP			60-80(16-27)	M		Barely cover seeds
Picea HT	★		55-60(13-16)	S	★	Erratic
Pilea GP			70-80(21-27)	S	★	Erratic. Keep moist
Pinus HT	★	★	55-60(13-16)	S	★	Erratic
Platycodon HP			65-70(18-21)	M	★	
Plumbago GSh			70-80(21-27)	M		Barely cover seed
Polemonium HP			65-70(18-21)	M		

Name[1]	Sow in autumn or pre-chill[2]	Pre-soak and/or chip seeds[3]	Germination temperature °F(C)[4]	Time taken to germinate[5]	Leave seeds uncovered[6]	Remarks
Polygonatum HP	★		50-60(10-16)	S/VS		May take two winters to germinate
Polygonum HHA, HP			65-70(18-21)	M/S		
Portulaca HHA			70-80(21-27)	M		Barely cover seeds outdoors. Surface sow under glass. Keep moist
Potentilla HP			65-70(18-21)	M		
Primula GP			60-65(16-18)	M		Keep cool in summer. Barely cover seeds
Primula HP	★		55-60(13-16)	M/S		Fresh seed may germinate rapidly; old seed erratic. Barely cover seeds. Keep moist
Prunus HT	★	★	65-75(18-24)	VS		Erratic. Best sown in autumn and left outdoors
Pseudotsuga HT	★		60-70(16-21)	S/VS	★	Erratic
Pulsatilla HP	★		60-70(18-21)	S/VS		Erratic. Do not overwater
Punica HHSh		★	65-70(18-21)	M/S		Erratic
Pyracantha HSh	★		50-55(10-13)	S/VS		Erratic. Stratify home-saved seeds
Pyrethrum HP			55-70(13-21)	M/S		Erratic
Ramonda HP			55-60(13-18)	S	★	Erratic
Ranunculus HP	★		50-60(10-18)	S		Erratic
Rechsteineria GBb			70-80(21-27)	S		

Name[1]	Sow in autumn or pre-chill[2]	Pre-soak and/or chip seeds[3]	Germination temperature °F(C)[4]	Time taken to germinate[5]	Leave seeds uncovered[6]	Remarks
Reseda HA			60-70(16-21)	M		Barely cover seeds. Best sown where to flower
Rhodanthe HHA			70-80(21-27)	M		Sow shallowly
Rhododendron HSh	★		55-65(13-18)	S	★	Erratic. Use lime-free compost. Shade seedlings from sun
Rhodohypoxis HP			50-60(10-16)	S		Erratic. Use lime-free compost
Rhus HSh		★	60-70(16-21)	S		
Ricinus HHA			65-70(18-21)	Q		Keep moist. Best sown in individual pots
Robinia HT		★	65-70(18-21)	M	★	Keep moist
Rochea HHP			65-75(18-24)	M/S	★	Keep moist
Rosa HSh	★		55-60(13-16)	S/VS		Erratic. Stratify home-saved seeds
Rudbeckia HHA			70-80(21-27)	Q/M		Barely cover seeds
Saintpaulia GP			70-80(21-27)	S	★	Erratic. Keep moist
Salpiglossis HHA			65-80(18-27)	M		Barely cover seeds
Salvia HA, HHA			65-70(18-21)	Q		Sow shallowly
Salvia, HP	★		60-70(16-21)	Q		
Santolina HSh			65-70(18-21)	M		
Sanvitalia HHA			65-75(18-24)	Q		Barely cover seeds. Best raised in individual pots
Saponaria HP			60-65(16-18)	M		Sow shallowly. High temperature may inhibit germination

Name[1]	Sow in autumn or pre-chill[2]	Pre-soak and/or chip seeds[3]	Germination temperature °F(C)[4]	Time taken to germinate[5]	Leave seeds uncovered[6]	Remarks
Saxifraga HP	★		60-70(16-21)	M/S		Erratic
Scabiosa HA			65-70(18-21)	Q		Do not sow early out of doors
Scabiosa HP			60-65(16-18)	M		Erratic
Schefflera GP			65-75(18-24)	M/S		Shade seedlings from sun
Schizanthus GA			60-65(16-18)	M		Barely cover seeds. High temperature may prevent germination
Scilla HBb	★		55-60(13-16)	S/VS		Erratic
Sedum HP	★		55-70(13-21)	M		Erratic. Sow shallowly
Sempervivum HP			55-70(13-21)	M		Erratic. Barely cover seeds
Senecio HHA			65-75(18-24)	M		
Sidalcea HP			50-60(10-16)	M/S		
Silybum HA			55-65(13-18)	M		
Smithiantha GP			65-80(18-27)	M	★	Mix seeds with sand. Keep moist
Solidago HP			55-70(13-21)	M/S		
Solanum GP			65-80(18-27)	M		Barely cover seeds. Move to frame for the summer
Sophora HT		★	70-80(21-27)	M		
Sparmannia GSh			65-80(18-27)	M		
Statice HHA			60-70(16-21)	Q		
Strelitzia GP		★	70-80(21-27)	S/VS	★	Erratic. Use well-drained compost but keep moist

Name[1]	Sow in autumn or pre-chill[2]	Pre-soak and/or chip seeds[3]	Germination temperature °F(C)[4]	Time taken to germinate[5]	Leave seeds uncovered[6]	Remarks
Streptocarpus GP			60-70(16-21)	M	★	Mix seeds with sand. Keep moist
Tagetes HHA			65-70(18-21)	Q		
Tellima HP	★		55-65(13-18)	S		Erratic
Teucrium HP			65-70(18-21)	M		Barely cover seeds
Thalictrum HP			55-65(13-18)	M		
Thuja HT	★		55-60(13-16)	S		Erratic
Thunbergia HHA			70-80(21-27)	M		Erratic. Best raised in individual pots
Thymus HP			55-65(13-18)	M/S	★	Keep moist
Tiarella HP	★		50-60(10-16)	S		Erratic
Tillandsia GP			65-75(18-24)	S		Sow shallowly
Tithonia HHA			70-80(21-27)	M		Best raised in small pots
Torenia GA			65-80(18-27)	M	★	
Trachelium HHA			65-75(18-24)	M		
Tradescantia HP			65-75(18-24)	S		
Trichosanthes HHA			65-75(18-24)	M		Sow in small pots
Trillium HP	★		60-70(16-21)	VS		Erratic. Requires two cooling periods to break dormancy. Barely cover seeds
Trollius HP	★		65-70(18-21)	S/VS		Erratic. Sow shallowly
Tsuga HT	★		55-65(13-18)	M/S	★	Erratic
Tulipa HBb	★		50-60(10-16)	S		Erratic

Name[1]	Sow in autumn or pre-chill[2]	Pre-soak and/or chip seeds[3]	Germination temperature °F(C)[4]	Time taken to germinate[5]	Leave seeds uncovered[6]	Remarks
Tweedia GP			70-80(21-27)	S		Erratic
Ursinia HHA			55-65(13-18)	M		Sow shallowly
Valerian HP			60-70(16-21)	M		
Venidium HHA			60-70(10-21)	Q		
Verbascum HB,HP			55-65(13-18)	M		
Verbena HHA			70-80(21-27)	M		
Verbena HP	★		60-70(16-21)	S		Erratic
Viburnum HSh	★		65-70(18-21)	VS		Erratic. Needs warm, cold, warm periods to trigger germination
Vinca GA			65-70(18-21)	M		
Viola HP			65-75(18-24)	M		
Viscaria HA			60-70(16-21)	M		
Vriesia GP			65-75(18-24)	M/S	★	Erratic
Wistaria HSh		★	55-65(13-18)	S		
Xeranthemum HA			65-70(18-21)	Q		
Yucca HP		★	65-75(18-24)	S/VS		Erratic
Zantedeschia HHP		★	75-80(24-27)	M/S	★	Erratic. Keep moist
Zea HHA			65-70(18-21)	Q		Sow in individual small pots
Zelkova HT	★		55-65(13-18)	S		Erratic
Zinnia HHA			65-75(18-24)	Q		Sow in individual small pots

FOOTNOTES TO APPENDIX 1

1 Names used are those in common use by seedsmen and are not necessarily the correct botanical one. Classification is according to plant use. Antirrhinum, for example, is really a perennial, but almost always treated as a half-hardy annual.

H = hardy   A = annual   P = perennial   HH = half-hardy   B = biennial   Sh = shrub
G = greenhouse   B b = bulb   T = tree

2 Expose sown containers to winter weather out of doors or place in a refrigerator for 6 weeks (see page 15).

3 Soak seeds in water that is hand warm to begin with. Sow any that swell: chip others or prick with a pin and re-soak (see page 12).

4 Temperatures shown are not the limits for germination, but the range likely to give good results.

5 Time taken to germinate varies according to treatment, but these are likely times under good conditions:
Q - within 14 days   M - up to 30 days   S - 30-90 days   VS - more than 90 days.

6 With very few exceptions, surface sown seeds are best germinated in good light.

† Erratic = seedlings appear sporadically and should be pricked out as they reach a suitable size.

Appendix 2

Hardy Annuals Suitable for Autumn Sowing Out of Doors

Adonis aestivalis (pheasant's eye)
Agrostemma
Alyssum maritimum
Asperula azurea setosa (annual woodruff)
Calendula (old English marigold)
Centaurea cyanus (cornflower)
Clarkia
Collinsia bicolor
Collomia
Convolvulus tricolor
Delphinium (larkspur)
Echium (viper's bugloss)
Erysimum perofskianum
Eschscholtzia (Californian poppy)
Gilia
Godetia
Gypsophila elegans
Iberis (candytuft)
Lathyrus odoratus (sweet pea)
Limnanthes douglasii
Linaria (toadflax)
Malcomia maritima (Virginian stock)
Nemophila (baby blue eyes)
Nigella (love-in-a-mist)
Omphalodes linifolia
Papaver rhoeas (Shirley poppy)
Salvia horminum (clary)
Saponaria vaccaria
Silene
Specular speculum (Venus's looking glass)

Appendix 3

Half-Hardy Annuals to Sow Direct in the Soil

Anagalis coerulea (pimpernel)
Balsam
Brachycombe (Swan river daisy)
Callistephus (China aster)
Gourds
Helychrysum (strawflower)
Matthiola (stocks)
Molucella (bells of Ireland)
Nolana
Phlox drummondii
Portulaca
Rhodanthe
Rudbeckia (cone flower)
Scabiosa
Tagetes (French and African marigolds)
Ursinia
Zinnia

Appendix 4
Sowing Season for Vegetables

Crop	Feb	March 1-15	March 16-31	April 1-15	April 16-30	May 1-15	May 16-31	June	July 1-15	July 16-31	August 1-15	August 16-31	Sept	Oct	Nov
Asparagus			S	S											
Asparagus pea					S	S									
Bean, broad	S/C	S/C	S	S	S										
Bean, French					C	C	S	S	S	X					
Bean, runner					C	C	S	S							
Beetroot, non-bolting	C	C	S	S	S	S	S	S	S	X	X				
Beetroot, maincrop					S	S	S	S	S	X	X				
Broccoli, sprouting							B	B							
Brussels sprouts	C	C	S	S											
Cabbage, spring										B	B				
Cabbage, summer	C	C	B	B	B	B									
Cabbage, winter						B	B	B							
Cabbage, red	C	C	B	B											
Calabrese					B	B	B	B							
Carrots	C	C	S	S	S	S	S	S	S	X	X				
Cauliflower, summer		C	B	B	B	B	B								
Cauliflower, winter						B	B								

See Footnote on page 194 for abbreviations.

Crop	Feb	March		April		May		June	July		August		Sept	Oct	Nov
		1-15	16-31	1-15	16-30	1-15	16-31		1-15	16-31	1-15	16-31			
Chicory, heading							S	S	X	X					
Chicory, forcing							S	S							
Cucumber					C	C	C	S							
Endive								S	S	X	X				
Globe artichoke						S	S								
Kale					S	S	S								
Kohl rabi	C	C	S	S	S	S	S	S	S	X	X				
Leek	C	C	S	S											
Lettuce, summer	C	C	S	S	S	S	S	S	S	S	X				
Lettuce, winter													X	C	
Marrow					C	C	S/C	S							
Onions, maincrop	C	C	S	S											
Onions, Japanese vars.												S			
Onion, spring	C	C	S	S	S	S	S	S	S	S	S		X		
Parsley		C	S	S				S	S						
Parsnips			S	S	S										
Peas, early dwarf	C	C	S	S	S	S	S	S							S
Peas, maincrop			S	S	S	S	S								
Pumpkin					C	C	S	S							
Radish, summer	C	C	S	S	S	S	S	S	S	S	S	X			

Crop	Feb	March		April		May		June	July		August		Sept	Oct	Nov
		1-15	16-31	1-15	16-30	1-15	16-31		1-15	16-31	1-15	16-31			
Radish, winter									S	S					
Salsify			S	S	S										
Savoy				B	B	B	B								
Scorzonera			S	S	S										
Seakale beet				S	S					S	S				
Spinach, summer	C	C	S	S	S	S	S								
Spinach, winter									S	S/X	X				
Squashes					C	C	S	S							
Swede						S	S	S							
Sweet corn					C	C	S/C	S							
Turnip, summer	C	C	S	S	S	S									
Turnip, winter									S	S/X	X				

C = sow under cloches S = sow in rows B = sow in seedbed for transplanting later X = sow in rows to be covered with cloches later

Times given are average and may need to be varied in the light of experience, taking into account such factors as locality, soil type, season and varieties used.

APPENDIX 5: What Went Wrong?

Outdoor Sowings

PROBLEM	CAUSE	CURE
No seedlings appeared (Inspect rows with great care to make sure that pests did not attack them as they emerged)	Soil too cold	Treat seeds with a seed dressing, especially for early sowings and slow-to-germinate kinds. Use cloches early in the season. Delay sowing until conditions suitable. Use fluid sowing technique
	Soil too hot - a problem that commonly affects soft-leaved lettuce in hot weather	Flood drills with cold water before sowing in late afternoon. Cover drills with boards for 48 hours after sowing. Use fluid sowing technique
	Seeds sown too deeply	Take care to adjust drill depth to suit seed being sown
	Seeds too old	Use fresh seed from a reputable source, especially for early sowings when conditions do not encourage swift germination
	Seeds need period of chilling to break dormancy	Keep area weed-free and moist and wait for another winter to pass. Make fresh sowing in a pot and chill in refrigerator if sufficient time available

PROBLEM	CAUSE	CURE
No seedlings appeared (Inspect rows with great care to make sure that pests did not attack them as they emerged)	Soil too dry at some stage	Flood drills with water before sowing. Firm soil over seeds to prevent rapid drying out. Keep drills moist where slow-germinating seeds are sown
	Seed coats impervious to water	Soak and/or chip seeds before sowing
Uneven germination - seedlings appear in groups here and there	Ill-prepared lumpy soil	Take more care over preparing the surface tilth, waiting until soil is suitable for working early in the year. Comb all stones and rubbish from the surface layer when raking
	Areas dried out	Water whole area a day or two in advance or flood drills immediately before sowing in dry weather. Firm soil over seeds along whole length of row
	Uneven drill depth	Pay attention to making drills of even depth
	Seeds attacked by soil pests	Usually occurs where the plot is newly prepared on fresh grassland, area of lawn or neglected, weedy plot. Work soil insecticide into site when preparing for sowing

PROBLEM	CAUSE	CURE
Uneven germination - seedlings appear in groups here and there	Soil capping	Hoe between rows to break up crust. Rake fine peat into soil surface when preparing seedbed. Keep surface soil moist to prevent seedlings being trapped beneath. Cover rows with cloches early in the season to prevent rain beating on the soil surface Make long-term improvement to humus content of soil by regular manuring
	Seeds removed by birds	Cover site with pea guards or small mesh netting
	Seeds removed by mice - look for neat funnel-shaped holes	Can be troublesome in early spring where peas and beans are sown. Put down traps or bait where birds and pets cannot get at them
Poor germination - seedlings appear sparsely along length of row	Seeds sown too thinly	Increase the number of seeds sown
	Ill-prepared soil	See above
	Soil too dry at some stage	See 'areas dried out'
	Seeds too old	See above
	Some seed coats impervious to water	See above

PROBLEM	CAUSE	CURE
Germination delayed	Soil too cold	Increase the number of seeds sown
	Soil too dry at some stage	See above
	Soil too hot	See above
	Seeds sown too deeply	See above
	Seed embryos incomplete	Sow a little earlier if this problem is expected. Cloches can speed development and emergence

TINY SEEDLINGS

PROBLEM	CAUSE	CURE
Stems shrivel at soil level and topple over	Damping off disease	Not usually a problem out of doors. Water drills and seedlings copiously with Cheshunt compound
Stems and leaves eaten off to ground level	Slugs and snails - look for silvery trails on plants/soil	Clear any rubbish and plant debris from the site. Put down slug bait and renew as necessary
	Woodlice	Clear any rubbish from site. Dust rows and along adjacent path edges, wall and fence bases with a suitable insecticide
	Mice	Put down traps or bait
Silvery puncture marks on leaves, development slow	Flea beetles - common on turnips and seedlings of the cabbage and beet families	Treat seeds with a seed dressing before sowing. Dust or spray rows of seedlings with derris

LARGER SEEDLINGS

PROBLEM	CAUSE	CURE
Uneven rounded edged holes in leaves	Slugs and snails - look for silvery trails or examine site with torch at night to find pests	Treat seeds with a seed dressing before sowing. Dust or spray rows of seedlings with derris
	Caterpillars - found by careful inspection of leaves	Pick off caterpillars if few or treat seedlings with a suitable insecticide
Jagged holes torn in leaves	Birds	Cover rows with netting or spray bird repellent
Plants collapse, stem eaten through at ground level	Cutworms	Scrape soil away to find dark caterpillar and destroy. Work soil insecticide into ground around seedlings and into fresh sites when preparing them for sowing. See 'seeds attacked by soil pests'
Growth slow, leaves puckered and distorted. Lice-like insects on undersides	Aphids	Treat rows with a suitable insecticide
Brassica plants wilt; tiny whitish grubs feeding on roots	Cabbage root fly	Treat seedbed at sowing time and all transplanted seedlings immediately with a suitable soil insecticide to ward off attacks
Plants eaten down close to soil level	Rabbits - look for tell-tale droppings	Fence plot with wire netting. Usually a problem only in rural gardens bordering open ground

Indoor Sowings

PROBLEM	CAUSE	CURE
No seedlings appear	Insufficient warmth	Check temperature requirements if known. Sow again in suitable conditions
	Too much heat	As above
	Covered too deeply	Check requirements if known. If not try re-sowing leaving half-uncovered, remainder barely covered and germinate in full light
	Seeds allowed to dry out at some stage	Water containers before or after sowing, firm the covering compost over the seeds or press seeds into surface, then put containers in clean plastic bags to keep them moist until germination occurs
	Seeds need period of chilling to break dormancy	Check requirements where known. Sow in autumn and expose to winter weather or chill for 6 weeks in a refrigerator after sowing. Beware of plants needing a warm period before chilling to trigger germination. Some, like eryngiums, may need artificial cold treatment more than once to start them off. A few need cold-warm-cold periods before they germinate
	Seeds too old	Resow, using fresh seeds

PROBLEM	CAUSE	CURE
No seedlings appear	Seeds coats impermeable to water	Soak and/or chip seeds before sowing
Uneven germination - seedlings appear in patches in containers	Seeds sown on uneven surface or covered unevenly	Take care to bring compost to a smooth, level surface before sowing and cover seeds with an even layer of soil
	Lumpy compost	Sift compost to remove fibrous rubbish and produce a finely broken sample to cover seeds
	Areas dried out	Make compost evenly firm, especially in seed trays, when preparing for sowing
	Seeds sown unevenly	Space sow seeds where possible. Mix tiny seeds with baked, fine sand to get even distribution
	Small seeds at or near the surface washed together by watering	Water containers before sowing. Any further watering best applied as a fine, misty spray
	Seeds removed by mice	Usually it is larger seeds that are taken. This can be a serious problem in a frame where birds, too, can be a nuisance. Cover containers with fine mesh netting. Put down traps where birds cannot be caught

PROBLEM	CAUSE	CURE
Poor germination - seedlings appear evenly but sparsely over whole container	Too few seeds sown	Sow more seeds
	Seeds too old or unviable	Obtain fresh seed from a reputable source and re-sow. Home-saved seeds of some species, such as arctotis, gazania and sanvitalia, can have low percentage of viability. Poor storage can also cause viability problems
	Variable germination inhibition	Prick out seedlings that appear, then fill holes in the seed container and keep moist over winter or give chilling treatment
	(Many of the causes listed under the previous two sections may result in poor germination where they are border-line cases. Too deep sowing, for example, may be just too deep for some seedlings, but others just struggle through)	

PROBLEM	CAUSE	CURE
Germination delayed	Insufficient warmth	Check temperature requirements and aim for optimum temperature for quick germination
	Too much heat	As above
	Seeds covered too deeply	Seedlings take longer to push through - adjust sowing depth
	Seeds too old	Use fresh seeds
	Compost too dry	Development delayed for lack of moisture. Water containers before or after sowing and keep moist
	Seed coast impermeable to water	Soak and/or chip seeds before sowing

TINY SEEDLINGS

Stems shrivel at soil level and topple over	Damping off disease	Water containers and seedlings with Cheshunt compound. Use clean containers and sterilised composts for future sowings
	Slugs and snails - look for silvery trails	Can be troublesome in frames especially. Clear away rubbish and plant debris that provide hiding places. Put down slug bait and repeat as necessary

PROBLEM	CAUSE	CURE
Eaten off at ground level	Woodlice	Frequently a problem in old structures where woodwork has started to rot. Clear away old boxes, pots and rubbish that provide shelter. Dust plants and likely hiding places with insecticide
	Mice - look for droppings	Usually troublesome only from autumn to spring. Keep structure in good repair and block up holes. Put down bait or traps where birds and pets cannot get at them
Seedlings yellow and sickly looking	Lack of air due to over-watering	Reduce frequency of watering. Allow soil to dry partially between waterings
	Over-wet soil due to poor drainage	Move seedlings into fresh compost. Pay special attention to giving adequate drainage layer in pots and boxes when using soil composts. Avoid over compressing peat composts
	Wrong compost	Use lime-free compost for acid-loving species

LARGER SEEDLINGS

PROBLEM	CAUSE	CURE
Leaves puckered or distorted, lice-like insects on undersides	Aphids	Spray, dust or fumigate with a suitable insecticide
Grey, fluffy mould developing on plants, especially at leaf edges, junction of leaves with stem, or on any bruised tissue	Botrytis (grey mould)	Remove and burn affected parts or whole seedlings if necessary. Reduce atmospheric humidity and avoid splashing water over plants. Spray or fumigate with suitable fungicide. Never leave dropped flowers, leaves or other plant debris lying about
Foliage yellow looking, growth falters	Over-watering	See 'lack of air' and 'over-wet compost'
	Starvation	Feed plants with balanced liquid fertiliser when they have spent 6 weeks in their containers or as soon as symptoms are noticed

Appendix 6

Planting Depths for Seeds

Sowing Outdoors

A. Surface and Just Cover - Grains
B. 1/8 in (25 mm) Liatris; Love-lies-bleeding (*Amaranthus caudatus*); Oriental Poppy; Portulaca
C. ¼ in (50 mm) Aquilegia; Convolvulous; Humulus
D. ½ in (1 cm) Calendula; Centaurea (Cornflower); Dimophotheca; Liatris; Linum grandiflorum; Zinnia; Lettuce; Onion; Radish; Spinach
E. ¾ in (1.5 cm) Cabbage; Carrot; Cucumber; Lavatera; Lupin; Radish; Spinach
F. 1 in (2 cm) Beetroot; Marrow (Squashes); Nasturtium; New Zealand Spinach; Parsnip; Pumpkin; Sweet Corn
G. 1¼ in (2.5 cm) Peas
H. 1½ in (4 cm) French Beans (Snap Beans)
I. 2 in (5 cm) Broad Beans(Fava Beans) ; Runner Beans

Sowing Indoors

A. Surface Sow - Begonia; Execum; Fern Spores; Lobelia
B. Just Cover - Campanula; Impatiens; Lettuce; Liatris
C. 1/8 in (25 cm) Aubergine (Egg Plant); Cabbage; Capsicum; Carnation; French and African Marigold; Tomato; Zinnia
D. ¼ in (50 mm) Asphodelus; Cyclamen; Pelagonium (geranium)
E. ½ in (1 cm) Cucumber; Garden Peas; Ipomoea; Sweet Peas; Ricinus
F. 1 in (2 cm) Broad Beans (Fava Beans); Runner Beans; Marrows (Squashes); New Zealand Spinach

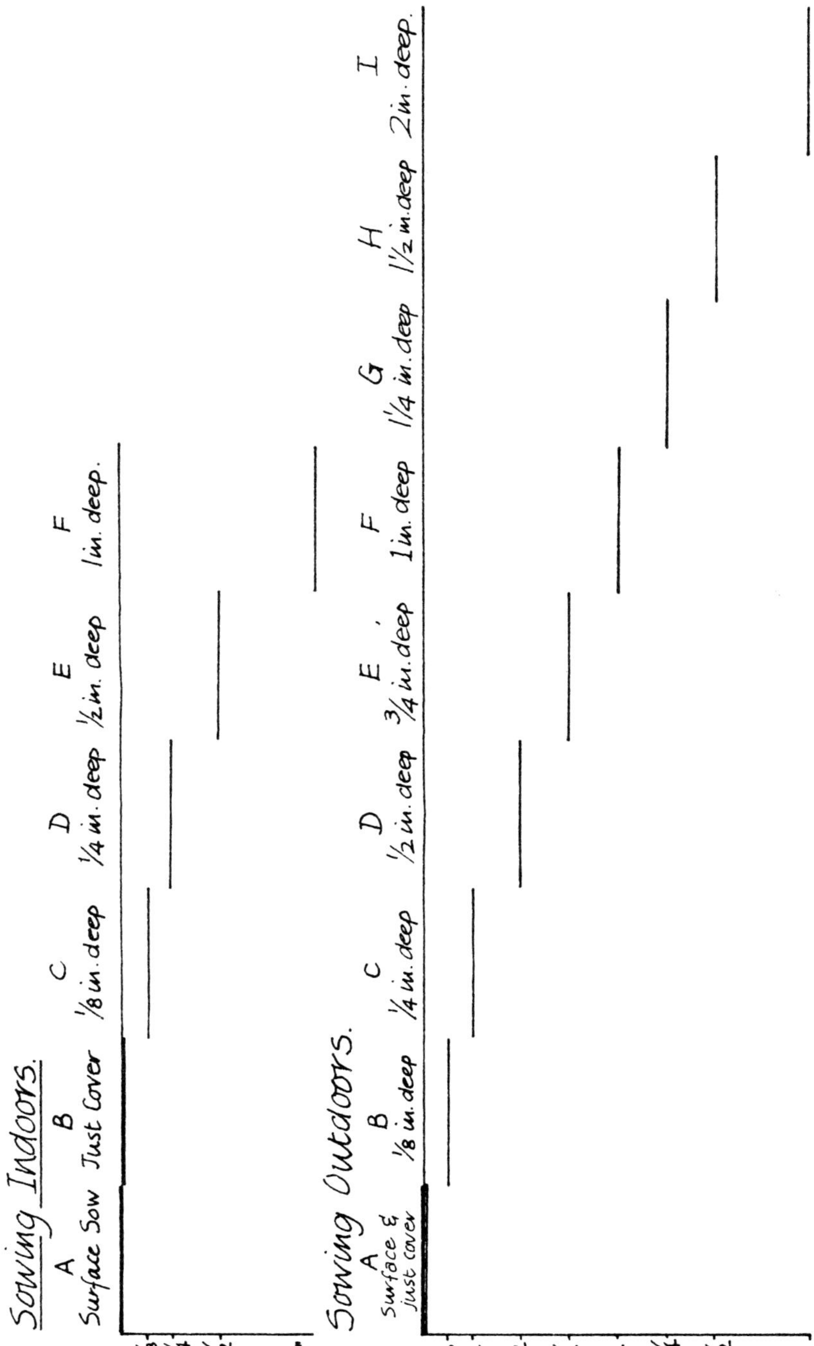
Sowing Indoors.
A Surface Sow
B Just Cover
C 1/8 in. deep
D 1/4 in. deep
E 1/2 in. deep
F 1 in. deep.
1/8
1/4
1/2
1"
Sowing Outdoors.
A Surface & just cover
B 1/8 in. deep
C 1/4 in. deep
D 1/2 in. deep
E 3/4 in. deep
F 1 in. deep
G 1 1/4 in. deep
H 1 1/2 in. deep
I 2 in. deep.
1/8
1/4
1/2
3/4
1
1 1/4
1 1/2
2

Appendix 7

Sources of Supply

Seeds

John Chambers, 15 Westleigh Road, Barton, Seagrave, Kettering, Northants, NN15 5AJ. - Specialist in seeds of native wild flowers, herbs, everlasting flowers and ornamental grasses. List free on request.

Chiltern Seeds, Bortree Stile, Ulverston, Cumbria, LA12 7PB - Very wide range of hardy and tender species from different areas of the world, as well as the more common ornamental plants. Vegetables restricted to a good list of Japanese kinds, together with a select selection of less common types.

Samuel Dobie & Son Ltd., Upper Dee Mills, Llangollen, Clwyd, LL20 85D. - Extensive seed range of greenhouse plants, flowers and vegetables including specialities. Some tree and shrubs, alpines and lawn seed, as well as seed raising equipment. Well illustrated and informative catalogue free on request.

Hurst's Seeds (Hurst, Gunson, Cooper & Tabor Ltd), Avenue Road, Witham, Essex. - Good general selection of vegetable and flower seeds.

Mommersteg International, Finedon, Wellingborough, Northants. - Interesting selection of 'Everlasting' flower seed collections and ornamental grasses for gardeners and flower arrangers, including immortelles, perpetuelles, thistle-like heads, fruits and seed pods.

Suffolk Herbs, Sawyers Farm, Little Cornard, Sudbury, Suffolk. - Wide selection of over 300 herbs and wild flower seeds. Seed list on request.

Suttons Seeds Ltd., Hele Street, Torquay, Devon, TQ2 7QJ. - Wide range of ornamental plant and vegetable seeds including herbs and lawn seed. Colourful and informative catalogue free on request.

Thompson & Morgan Ltd., London Road, Ipswich, Suffolk, IP2 0BA. - One of the longest seed lists including many trees, shrubs, bulbs and exotic greenhouse plants as well as more popular flowers and vegetables. Catalogue free on request.

Unwins Seeds Ltd., Histon, Cambridge, CB4 4LE. - Excellent list of vegetables and flowers including house plants, trees and shrubs. Sweet peas a speciality. Extensively illustrated catalogue free on request.

Specialist Societies: There are a number of specialist societies, such as the Hardy Plant Society and Alpine Garden Society, that are often sources of unusual seeds in their own particular fields, either direct from the Society or from fellow members. Their publications can be an important source of information to anyone aiming to raise their own plants.

Royal Horticultural Society: Once a year there is a free distribution of surplus seeds from the RHS Garden at Wisley to members who apply to be included in the scheme. This is a valuable source of many rare plants and shrubs that would be difficult to obtain by other means, as well as covering more common species.

Equipment

Access Irrigation Ltd., Crick, Northampton, NN6 7XS. - Range of glass sided, aluminium garden frames, some equipped for mist watering; also frame heaters.

Bayliss Autovents Ltd., Compton Street, Ashbourne, Derbyshire, DE6 1DA. - Specialist manufacturers of automatic greenhouse ventilation controls.

Bentall Simplex Ltd., Maldon, Essex, CM9 7NW. - Greenhouses and frames; soil and space heaters; automatic ventilation, watering and misting equipment; electric propagators and plant lamps.

The Fyba Pot Company, Malvern Road, Knottingley, W. Yorks. - Fyba propagation systems, including peat pots, containing fertiliser for roots of germinating seeds, and Growtubes for sweet peas, beans and peas, etc.

Jiffy Pot (UK) Ltd, Croft Chambers, Croft Road, Crowborough, East Sussex. - Rich peat pots - impregnated with plant food to promote vigorous and early root action - in a wide range of sizes, and packs of expanding Jiffy-7 pots.

Macpenny International Ltd., Gore Road Industrial Estate, New Milton, Hampshire. BH25 6SF. - Humex range of propagators and growing chambers, automatic watering misting and ventilation equipment, heaters, electric control equipment and greenhouse blinds.

Two Wests and Elliott Ltd., Unit 4, Carrwood Road, Sheepbridge Industrial Estate, Chesterfield, Derbyshire, S41 9RH. - Greenhouse staging, benches and shelving; automatic watering systems, fans, heaters, plant lamps, propagators, cloches and frames.

Index

Numbers in italics refer to illustrations